COSMOPOLITAN
THE LETTERS YOU ALWA

COSMOPOLITAN
THE LETTERS YOU ALWAYS
WANTED TO WRITE

Edited and with an Introduction by
Marcelle d'Argy Smith

A Robin Clark Book
London

First published in Great Britain in 1986 by
Robin Clark Ltd
A member of the Namara Group
27/29 Goodge Street
London W1P 1FD

British Library Cataloguing in Publication Data

Cosmopolitan: the letters you always wanted to write.
1. English letters
I. Smith, Marcelle d'Argy
826'.914'08   PR1347

ISBN 0-86072-108-6

Typeset by Reprotype, Peterborough
Reproduced, printed and bound in Great Britain by
Hazell Watson & Viney Limited,
Member of the BPCC Group,
Aylesbury, Bucks

TABLE OF CONTENTS

INTRODUCTION

It is quite extraordinary how much does not get said in a lifetime of interaction with others. Those words, sentences which are fully formed and jostling around in your brain, are all too often not expressed to the person for whom they are intended.

With good and prudent reason in some cases. Would it really serve a purpose to tell an ex-lover what you thought of him? Might it not upset a carefully arranged life to contact a person you once knew to tell them how often you think about them? Is it worth telling your boss, your bank manager, your best friend or the other woman how angry and upset you are?

Sometimes it's a question of pride, dignity. And the spoken word, even if carefully rehearsed, has a strange habit of taking conversational twists and turns you never intended. When you're talking with someone, their reactions may confuse you, their responses may deflect you from your intended speech. But how often have you said later to a friend, 'Oh I was dying to say what I *really* thought'?

It's part of being socialized – and for socialized read repressed – that makes us keep our thoughts and emotions to ourselves. Where love is concerned it seems to be especially difficult to convey the depths of our feeling. It would seem like a dramatic declaration, so embarrassingly out of place in our everyday lives, to tell a partner, a parent, a precious child how much they truly mean to us. Even if you do hug someone close and say, 'You've no idea how much I love you', you somehow have the feeling that they *don't* know, they can't even begin to grasp the enormity of your emotion.

And yet, have you noticed that such inhibitions, fears of rejection, fears of appearing foolish, fears of saying what is on your mind, so often vanish completely when you sit down to write a letter? You can measure your words, write and re-write if necessary. You can be wonderfully loving, bitterly cross or terribly funny because you've had time to think about it and the person you're addressing can't interrupt you. You need more discipline but less courage because letter-writing isn't confrontational.

But even some *letters* take guts. 'I'm leaving' rarely comes easily and probably takes a good deal of soul-searching before it gets put on paper. 'I love you' with a couple of pages of explanation feels so *good* to write – even if it's a confession. It's marvellous to have the space to tell someone. And most of us rather like written emotions – whereas in truth we, too, might shy away from being told to our face.

The letters that truly hit home are the honest ones. In a world where so much social and personal hypocrisy is considered acceptable, even necessary, an honest sentiment shines as brilliantly as the North Star. Sometimes these letters get written but they don't get posted. Or they do, and as any postman will tell you he has encountered at least one person on his rounds who is pleading with him outside someone's front door saying, '*Please* don't deliver that letter. I wrote it and I've changed my mind. *Please* can I have it back.'

Tricky one that. In law, once you have posted a letter it becomes the property of the Post Office until it is delivered. It's not known how many postmen take pity on the writers.

But sometimes you feel better just for the writing. You're forced to consider what you feel and often the act of unburdening yourself on paper helps you to reassess. Often you're aching for someone to know that despite your vulnerability or anger you're a funny girl, a survivor with a sense of humour. And humour is a terrific way of getting a point across in a letter.

A few months ago *Cosmopolitan* asked readers to write 'The letter you've always wanted to write'. It was the letter they'd put off writing, hadn't dared to write, had meant to but somehow had left too late. We wanted letters that were 'refreshing, original, but above all honest'. The response, and the quality of the response, was staggering. I can only describe it as a torrent of emotion as the letters came in by the sackload. Words written with passion, humour, warmth, sadness, gratitude, joy and love.

At the time I remember staring at people at bus stops in Oxford Street as I waited for the number 15 thinking, as I looked at total strangers, 'I wonder if all that bottled up feeling is inside of *you*?' And I guessed it was.

It was touching that people, our readers, would reveal so much of themselves and send the letters to us. A few had covering letters that said, 'Dear *Cosmo*, please send this back when you've read it.' A couple said, 'Dear *Cosmo*, this is so personal that I request your absolute confidentiality' – which they have, of course. And some said, 'Dear *Cosmo*, thank you. I so enjoyed writing this letter.'

We decided that some of the letters were too good simply to end up on our files. Would it be possible, we wondered, to put them in a book? And so we wrote to a hundred of our letter-writers asking if we could print their letters and also asking if names should be used.

The overwhelming majority said they'd be delighted and as one writer put it, 'If the other letters are as honest as mine, I can't *wait* to read the book.'

Over to you. We hope that you'll get the same pleasure from reading them as we did. Personally speaking, I can tell you I'm thrilled to have these letters after my name.

Marcelle d'Argy Smith
Features Editor, *Cosmopolitan* Magazine

LOVERS AND MARRIAGE

Madeleine,

If there's one thing I have missed in all the time I have known you, it's letters. It might sound daft to you but I always wanted to write to you about all the things I think of when I am away on my own. When we met, we saw each other so often, and living pretty close to each other, I didn't take the time to write. Then we moved in together into the little flat above the hairdresser's shortly after. Remember those cold nights without heating! And you getting into bed dressed like Chris Bonnington! Me trying to be the hero wearing nothing except a brave grin. Different today, I am in Bali with the temperature in the high eighties. It's a dream place and the only improvement to this beautiful island would be your company. As I look out to sea I can feel us making love on these silky sands. Oh if only! It's funny, the things that run through your mind just day-dreaming. After the breaking-up of my marriage I trusted no one and lived an almost hermit lifestyle; then I met you by chance and I was like a kid again and fell madly in love with you. I was so scared at first. I just couldn't believe what was happening. And now, the few years we have been together have been so rich in love that if you left today the memories would fill a lifetime. My life would be shattered for sure because I am certain that a person can love and be loved like this only once. I value every moment with and without you. I have never made love like I have made love with you. Like fantasies and wild imaginings, you came from nowhere, and the magic in the moments when we touch are there for all to see. More fulfilled, a man could not be. I will try to make every day a new day for us, even if I do poke my big nose into your cooking – interfering sod that I am. And I'll try not to scratch the pans again. Bertie Bungle here! I suppose I worry sometimes about our

1

age difference and I don't know why, perhaps it's just me being stupid. I only hope I can always make you happy. I am in love with you so much Madeleine. Oh, if only I could just touch you, how complete I would feel right now. The sun is setting and my temperature is rising fast. I will have to try and stop my thoughts getting the better of me. I look forward so much to cuddling up to you again soon and feeling your warmth. Keep smiling and miss me, a bit. And just for the record! Marrying you was the best thing that ever happened to me.

All my love,
N

Dear Elizabeth,

I don't suppose for one moment of your wildest dreams you anticipated my writing. And had I not seen a competition in a magazine rewarding an interesting letter with a holiday for two worth £5000 I doubt the idea of sending you a letter would have occurred to me, but the 1/1000000 chance that I might win – I'm afraid at your expense emotionally because they usually print the winner; and at my gain emotionally because I'd take Jonas with me to Penang (the Jewel of the Orient as it is known) – was too provocative to resist. Also it was an opportunity, an attempt to try to tell you how ambivalent I am about the situation we three find ourselves in as from yesterday: Sunday when Jonas moved out.

I can barely imagine how you must be feeling. Stockholm is one hour ahead of us so whilst you are thinking in early evening terms of bathing the children I am still late working afternoon waiting for a call from Malaysia to say whether the tour of *Hamlet* there in December is on or off. They are 8 hours ahead of my problems: my ambivalence already shows with regard to my work. Six months ago I would have dreaded a 'no thanks' from them, after all I've pushed and shoved to tour Shakespeare in the Far East for nearly two years – fought to raise the money and interest. Today I dread them saying 'yes please' because it would mean 3 months missing Jonas, missing him and wondering about his sexual abstinence and mine for that matter! If I go I risk losing him, if I stay I fail my ambitions. So what is more important? HIS WIFE! HIS CHILDREN! HIS RESPONSIBILITIES! you scream at me as you come through your first whole day 7 hours behind Malaysia without your husband.

Elizabeth, I know he moved out because I finally said 'choose' but we were all going crazy with uncertainty. I knew I couldn't keep flying to Paris, Amsterdam, Ibiza, Rome and Stockholm (x 6) to spend any more hot and wonderful nights in different hotel beds with him – did you know we have a collection of 23 various hotel beds since it all started in my bed last February? It was lunatic and it was not burning out which is what we all were praying for: each time we said goodbye it proved a greater wrench than the time before. So someone had to do something. He was waiting for you to kick him out and after the third time you let him go to me I knew you never would; so he left because I refused to sob at airports anymore. I am also certain in my heart that he left not because I am so irresistible but because your marriage had broken down. There's the rub, Elizabeth, and you may well tear this letter up and spit in my third eye: it is not all my fault nor his. He left because I am not a saint, because I love making love with him and making him laugh – you didn't and I am not sure that your very pronounced views on the 'shoulds' and 'oughts' in your pretty little neighbourhood actually mean much when it comes to 'needs' and 'loving' – that is for you to find out now you are on your own. It is hard work living with a saint, you made him feel permanently guilty for being him. He didn't much like it; it must be like waking up every morning with a heavy hangover of the soul and you standing there looking like the dose of salts . . . not much fun methinks day after day.

But please don't think I am sitting here gloating over having stolen your beautiful husband. I feel a frightened fool ever to have dabbled my varnished toes into this particular water. Why you may ask? Well, I can already see a dreadful trap emerging – Jonas is quixotic, devastatingly attractive and unselfconsciously curious about everything. After 16 years of curbing his curiosity in pretty stolid marriage – with good behaviour brownie points – I fear that through me he is just beginning to learn that he has a lot of adventure, pleasure to catch up on. He's an awfully willing pupil and very good at it, so what happens to me in 5 years' time when he's exhausted my sixth-form skills of Life and some other 'adventure' lures him into her bed? By this time now I am 40 and childless (oh yes, he has made it quite clear he doesn't want any more children). That will be my happiness over and I'll be out (I can see you crying into your gin and tonic no, sorry, I forgot – you are a teetotaller *and* a stoic . . .)

I have no choice now, I love him and I must face up to my responsibility (dreadful word) for what I have made happen. You will have to face up to yours (a little more leniently this time I hope) and Jonas will never have to because there will always be enough damn women out there who will do to me what I have done to you. No question.

It is very disconcerting to have one's heart's desire granted you know . . . considering I never wanted him to begin with! Jonas was nothing but my schoolfriend's gorgeous, deadly serious, and irreproachable husband. I nearly fell over with shock the first moment I realized that he was flirting with me. I can't stand actors as lovers – I know too much about their stupefying narcissism to be impressed – and I never wanted another foreigner – you know all that remains of my affairs with Americans, Germans, Dutch and the Brazilian are the huge telephone bills! – the only tangible evidence that we did talk hours across oceans – because believe me 99% of the conversation you cannot begin to remember. So, my dear, I did not set my cap at your beautiful Swedish Film-Star Husband, he was the last thing I was looking for . . .

What will happen? God knows. Rest assured he won't ever come back to you but don't think that I am his final resting place either. So as unhappy as no doubt you are now, two things: It's no triumphant bed (of roses) here and if and when your two little girls come and stay with us I shall be as supportive of you as you could wish. I hope you can spare me some compassion after you have retched up all the bile of bitterness. Life is not Fair.

Your ex-friend,
Flora

(Ms Fiona Gaunt)

Dear Petra,

Allow me to introduce myself. You see, I am the other woman in your husband's life. I'm sure that you know by now that I exist, goodness knows Charles has stayed away from home enough times for even you to suspect something. I will come straight to the point. Why don't you divorce him? He owes you absolutely nothing and I am well aware that you certainly don't need him any more. The sad truth is that I do! You see I have all the time in the world to listen to him when he's hurting. The strange thing is that it's all about you and how dedicated you are to your tiresome duty. Can't you see what is happening? Don't you worry when he doesn't come home at nights? If he were my husband, I would not sleep until he was in bed beside me. Petra dear, modelling isn't a career, it's a sworn duty. You have to forget all about your family and friends and be there when you are needed. Don't you realize that Charles was never used to being treated that way? I am only writing to you because I happen to love your husband very much and I want to give you a chance to defend your actions.

For what it's worth he has told me that he loves me too, but we are so close that I think I already knew it. I can tell by the way he looks at me when we are sitting together silently in the firelight. But perhaps I've always known that his love for you was far greater than his love for me. That's why it hurts so much that I can hardly sleep at night. However, I've got a part of him that you can never touch!

I think I would like to meet you again, Petra. It's been a very long time since I last looked into those cold stone-coloured eyes of yours. I know the truth you see. I know what is causing the rift between you and Charles. You're too successful, too diligent, too dedicated. Why do you grieve him so? Why, Petra? It breaks my heart to love him so much and to see you hurting him in the way that you do. Have you a heart of stone? I've offered to have him come and live with me but he is still waiting for you. One day he will tire of that and then I will have him back so quickly you won't believe it. He says he will wait, but wait for what? Wait until you give up modelling and become a good wife to him? Wait until you change? Can a leopard change its spots? Or perhaps he means he will wait until you've broken him completely, until you've so totally emasculated him that he won't have the guts to leave you. Yes, that's really what you would like isn't it, Petra?

Charles stayed last night. How lovely it was to have breakfast together this morning. We got up early and I made pancakes which we ate off the same plate in front of the fire with maple syrup and fresh whipped double cream, sheer luxury. We also chatted for a while about old times and how we both wished we could turn the clocks back to that time. We giggled sinfully as we indulged ourselves in the deliciously fattening pancakes. When it was time to go I walked him to the door and he kissed me gently and strode off down the garden path stopping briefly to stroke Skittle as she made her way home after a long night hunting fieldmice in the fields beyond the house. He lingered for a few seconds at the gate and looked back as if he desperately wanted to say something but just couldn't find the right words. My foolish heart beat in anticipation but he seemed to falter, than changed his mind and blew me another kiss instead as he climbed into his silvery grey sports car and set off into the day leaving me fulfilled and ecstatically happy. But for the nagging thought at the back of my mind that tonight he would be with you again.

Last week was different. He dropped me at work after breakfast and I climbed proudly out of the car as I instinctively felt everyone watching us together. His dark head and my fair head came together for one last fleeting kiss and then I watched pensively as he set off for the office. The girls all wanted to know who that tall dark handsome stranger was and I was proud to annouce that it was Charles. Are you proud of him, Petra? Do you love him like I do? Does your heart ache when you say goodbye each day or are you in too much of a hurry to get under the bright lights and have people admiring you? Charles arrived last weekend with his arms laden with fresh white roses. I must admit that I cried just a little bit. I graciously accepted them even though in my heart I knew they had been bought with you in mind. It hurts to play second best but then perhaps some day you will realize just how much. I am not usually malicious but I hope you will understand one day, Petra.

If I sound bitter it's probably because I am. I never was any good at hiding my feelings. Why did you choose to marry him when you knew even at that time that you were hopelessly dedicated to and in love with your own job? You never realized that you would be competing with me for his affections. Petra, the last thing I want to do is hurt you but I feel you should know these things and I really don't want anyone else to tell you. If you are already aware of the dangers then this letter will only serve to reinforce that awareness but if you are not then you must be either blind or else you just don't want to face facts. Your marriage is melting away before your very eyes and I don't think you even care. Why oh why is there no justice in this cruel world? You are so talented and so beautiful and you also have Charles eating out of your hand while I am plain and unworthy of the attention that Charles lavishes upon me so generously. But I do know that I have his love and his unending devotion, no matter what may happen. Can you be sure of that, Petra? I've tried so hard not to meddle in your affairs but I know beyond all shadow of doubt that I could give him all the love and care that a man like Charles thrives on.

I feel this will serve only to infuriate you but I want you to know everything and if I have omitted to say anything which you feel might be important I would be quite prepared to meet you to discuss it.

People say that your love is different from mine but so what? It's still love isn't it, Petra? When we were growing up we had such plans for how we were going to live together and always be happy but that was before you came along and spoiled it all. You stole his heart, not from him because he had long since parted with it, but from me. I was his first and only true love. I think I've said all I want to say now but I could not finish off this letter without telling you who I am. You see I am Susan, Charles' sister. I do love him with all my heart and I was the one who looked after him when he was being bullied at school. I was the one who dried his tears and I suppose I still am. That's why, Petra. That's why I cannot go on letting you hurt him, because I still feel responsible for him and I guess I always will. When Charles hurts, I hurt. It has always been that way and I don't think it is likely to change now. I hope this goes a long way to explaining the love I have for my brother. I cannot let you go on hurting him. I hope you understand. I hope that in the near future you will find a way to

change and become what he wants you to be or you are in grave
danger of losing a very precious, very rare and beautiful man.

Yours,
Susan

(Mrs Norma H. McVitty)

My dear Husband,

I had a very pleasant journey here, the roads were not too busy, and the car ran beautifully.

It is such a long time since I wrote a letter to you. The reason I am writing now is because I was unable to telephone. I am told that the phone in Julia's new home will be fixed within a day or two, so I'm looking forward to being able to talk to you then. I tried to telephone you from the local public telephone box, but, alas, it had been vandalized. It will be nice to talk to you and to be able to tell you how well your grandson is progressing.

I'm kept busy as you can imagine. The two toddlers need some looking after, as they soon get into mischief. They are delightful, and keep asking me how Grandpa is, and if he has stayed at home to look after his tomatoes! Mother and the new baby are easy to attend to, because they stay in the same place where I put them. It is most enjoyable taking care of them, and I'm loving every minute. However, when they are all safely tucked up in bed, and the house goes quiet. I begin to miss you such a lot.

This situation reminds me of the war years, when we had to be parted. Six and a half years was such a very big slice out of our lives, when, like so many others, we were conscripted into the armed services. At the beginning of the war, we thought it would be over very quickly. What a forlorn hope! We used to write to each other every day, although the letters didn't always arrive in the order in which they were posted, but your passionate letters kept me going.

Eventually, the dreaded day arrived, and we shared your embarkation leave together. That was wonderful, but oh! the agony of yet another parting, and your setting sail for goodness knows where. The number of letters I continued to write, addressed to ROZGH – not knowing where you were for weeks and weeks. I imagine you received them all together when you finally reached your destination.

The letters you sent me from India were extremely interesting. It seemed as if you were talking to me; it was a different world you were telling me about. In England, in those days, we were not accustomed to seeing women dressed in sarees, and men wearing turbans, and we knew nothing of Indian customs.

I thought when VJ Day was proclaimed, you would probably

decide to carry on in the Royal Signals, as you seemed to enjoy life as an officer out there. I began to hope that you would ask me to come and join you, and I was beginning to feel some excitement at the prospect of living a lazy life with servants, having listened to glowing reports from some of my friends.

This never materialized as you could see that living in India wasn't going to be the same in peace time. Already there was talk of losing part of the Commonwealth, and you just couldn't wait to come back to dear old England quick enough.

When at last we were able to start our lives together, once again we were dealt a cruel blow. The results of your examinations earned you quick promotion in 'civvy street', and once again we were parted as you were sent to London to work. We survived all this, and eventually we were able to bring up our family as a joint affair. I think it was all worth waiting for, and I've been very lucky in having you for a husband.

Now our children are adults, and it seems to me we are getting even more pleasure from our grandchildren, then we did from our own children. Perhaps it's because we don't have the same responsibility for their upbringing. All this reminiscing is a clear sign that we are growing old, but how lovely it has been so far, and what a good life we've made of it with all our voluntary activities to make it more interesting and rewarding for us.

So it's our children and grandchildren's turn, and I hope they are going to be as happy as we are.

Do take care of yourself whilst I'm not there to look after you.

Your ever loving wife,
Hilda

(Mrs Hilda Firth)

My very dear Jay,

When I got your call last week my heart almost stopped, and my voice felt as if it belonged to someone else, I was so terrified of saying the wrong thing, that I am sure that you must have thought that I had lost my senses. You asked me to come, so here I am, in your city, and although I should be totally exhausted after such a long flight, instead, I have decided to walk by the sea, breathe the heavy warm air and think . . . if only I could think.

You must have sat here on this wall looking at the beach many times . . . there are so many beautiful women here . . . why did you want ME to come? The Pacific is calm but grey, and the wind is blowing my hair into my face . . . will you recognize the new, more 'American', me . . .

Was I wrong to travel so far?

How can I sleep or eat when tomorrow we will see each other again after two years.

Only 2 years but to me every day was that long apart from you . . . I know, I was always so cool . . . did you never really suspect that I was in a turmoil absolutely alien to my 'so English' way of life? For those days when we were together I thought that I was living in another world, and I was.

Which way was up?

Why did I not suspect that you felt the same way too. I could not believe that you, such a superstar, would be interested in me . . . who?

Do you remember you once told me that you met so many people each day that you often could not remember their names? You made me think that I should never, in any way, express interest in how you felt even when I knew that you needed me, just to talk to . . . and now, today, I can hardly believe that I am here . . . and that everything has changed so fast . . .

Pelicans . . . aren't they funny, why were they made so ugly and yet so beautiful at the same time. But now everything is beautiful, those clouds, the trees, the grey sea, my tiredness, my hunger . . . am I hungry?

I love you.

Will I dare to tell you tomorrow?

Will I be able to speak?

If I were a novel heroine, or an actress, my lines would be

written, and so would yours, we would know how to act, and what to say. But this isn't about acting, so how will our film end?

Well, even Santa Monica is reality for some of those people on the beach and my reality is that I have got to get up off this wall before I have its pattern etched on my skin forever.

Tomorrow: how will it end?...how will it begin?...

But aren't all our ends new beginnings?

Will we take our first steps to a new end together in the sun tomorrow? Will we dare?

Dearest Peregrine,

Have arrived safely and thought I'd better keep you posted. Of course I didn't resent your suggestion that I ought to lose a pound or two. No, I'm not sulking. I should simply hate not to be a credit to you. It was really very sweet of you to pay for me to come here, rather than waste your money on a silly old engagement ring... That's one of the things I most admire about you, dearest Perry, you are a man of logic whose priorities are so well defined.

When I arrived I found they'd booked me into two rooms, presumably to accommodate the overspill... The room is vast (for the same reason no doubt), all bamboo and smoked glass. Even the bathroom mirrors are heavily smoked, which means that one can only see 'through a glass but darkly'. I expect this is considered a kindness, so's we can't view the full horror of our bodies with any clarity.

Friday After breakfasting on black coffee, went off to face my first ordeal – the Dietician. Waited outside her door and felt as though I was under threat of six of the best from the headmistress.

The lady herself, a Miss Bantam, belied her puny name, and rose a formidable six feet to greet me. Personally, I thought her a very poor advertisement for good nutrition. The buttons of her snowy-white overall were straining across her ample bosom, creaking their protest in the fierce starch. She kept saying 'we' all the time. 'We'll just hop on the scales and we'll weigh you.' Wouldn't have been room for both of us I thought dourly. She announced my weight with a deep sigh and sat down with heavy, and I mean heavy, resignation. 'Well, we seem to have quite a bit of work to do, don't we?'

We eyed each other glassily across the desk, and she then, with relish, produced a diet born of pure malice.

I had to cheer myself up after this ordeal, so I adjourned to the Hawaiian bar and ordered a Florida Frolic, which turned out to be lemon juice and soda water. Whilst sipping this, I frolicked through the list of special treatments.

Saturday I feel *much* thinner today. This could be because there are so many fat people around that I look positively anorexic. Personally, I think I must need building up and cherishing. Are you sure I need to lose weight, Peregrine dear? Of course I shall bow to your superior judgement on the matter, but I'm sure you would view my bulges in a different light if only you could see the comparison for yourself.

Sunday The days are so busy here. The place is full of hurtling jogging suits and dressing gowns, all scuttling off to their next appointment. I had a most diverting treatment today. I lay naked on a bed of foil, then this girl advanced upon me, weilding a bucket of hot wax and a huge distemper brush. She slapped hot wax all over me, then carefully made a foil parcel of me. Felt as though I was marinading, ready for the barbecue.

Monday I am turning a most curious colour. Red and brown from the sun treatments, and black and blue from the massages. They can get quite vicious, and the cubicles during massage sessions resound with slapping, shrieking and groaning.

Tuesday A very nice lady felt my feet today and told me I had a headache. Awfully clever, I thought, knowing I had a headache from rolling my big toe around. Of course, it could have been my pained expression that gave the game away.

Wednesday Weight is positively melting away. I have joined the exercise class. Twenty female fatties perched on excruciatingly narrow bicycle saddles, peddle furiously away. Much more peaceful is the yoga. Feel so calm, I almost levitated out of the gym.

Thursday Thank you for your letter Peregrine. I would have posted this before now, only I met with a little trouble. I decided a stroll to the nearest letter box would do me good. My outdoor mufti was obviously viewed with deep suspicion. I was followed all the way down the drive by a large female bouncer. Felt like a wanted KGB agent. Anyway, I got bounced back in, your letter still in my hand.

Had to take my jaded nerves to the jacuzzi. This is the recognized place for a good moan. Has rather a Roman baths atmosphere, communal bathing whilst discussing the day's events. It can be tricky to stay perched on one's ledge with the full force of a high pressure water jet playing between one's shoulder blades. Protagonists frequently disappear in mid-flow as it were, which rather has the effect of spoiling their argument.

Friday Well, only one more day. I think you'll see a big change in me Perry. Had wonderful treatments all day. Only two unpleasant ones. I was attacked by a sink plunger to break down my fatty tissues. Left a broken woman, so it must be working.

In true masochistic fashion, I followed this with a bikini wax, in readiness for our holiday. Having had the necessary area waxed, they chatted away in a most companionable manner. I was beginning to think that there really was nothing to this, and couldn't imagine what all the fuss had been about, when the kiss of Judas, *et tu Brute*, and all that. My attention was drawn to the autumnal tints of the trees, and as I turned my head to gaze out, they yanked off the wax and half of me. Later they peeled me off the ceiling.

Tonight I am going to my final class on self-assertion. Feel far from self-assertive after my ordeal. I am not so much waxing lyrical, as waxing fearful. Soon be home Peregrine my darling.

Saturday The self-assertion class was most stimulating and revealing. I am a changed woman now, outwardly and inwardly.

Last night I learnt a new word. I learnt to say 'NO'. I am going to practise it on you Perry. 'NO' 'NO' 'NO'.

I am not going to marry you. How dare you suggest I need to lose weight, you self-opinionated, scrawny chauvinist. If you don't care for me the way I am, then, *'tough'*. You're a stuffy, overbearing, callous prig.

I'm sorry, because I know that you've put a lot of work in on me. I speak as you wish, have my hair according to your dictates, wear the clothes you like, entertain only the people who can further your career, have changed my hobbies, reading habits and even my body to seek your approval.

I shall be exactly what I want to be. So go find yourself another amorphous human lump of modelling clay and get to work.

> Yours assertively,
> Octavia

> (Hilary Rochford Dyer)

Ma Chère Hélène,

Do you remember me? It is now five years since we met that April morning on Quai Branly beside the Seine. You were walking in front of me when your shopping bag split open, spilling the contents to the ground. I stopped to help you in your embarrassment. Leaving the smashed eggs to one side, we gathered the provisions in a heap and pondered the next move. We were bagless. I said, 'What about a call to arms?' You laughed and, scooping up the flotsam, I silently offered mine.

You remember me now? We travelled together along the Quai D'Orsay to Blvd Saint-Germain discussing the difficulty of obtaining strong paper receptacles in a world of plastics, the potential of an unbreakable eggshell, and, of course, Paris in the Spring. Our gestures were few: our arms were full of tomatoes, jambon, vin and pain. You led the way. I made a bold attempt to take the lead at the Musée de Cluny crossing, looking right instead of left, and was narrowly saved from the jaws of a Renault van by your grabbing, grasping hands. That little episode resulted in our bagless load ending up in the gutter. Catching my contrite eyes, you laughed and laughed again. It was at that moment that I fell in love with you.

Back in your fifth-floor appartment in Rue des Plantes, near the Latin Quarter we sipped café au lait and ate croissants and talked on and on about philosophy, politics and phobias – the three p's. You were a follower of Mauriac, whose stress on ineffectual guilt and spiritual gloom – I remember you saying – was also found in Julian Green and George Bernanos and in Henri Bosco's *Mas Théotime*. You hated the Cylindrical Movement and its rational nihilism, as well as Kant and all his mad categories. We drank vin rouge, laughing at the foibles of our age and the mad histories of our respective countries. Religion, archaeology, nationalism, cinema, snails – we covered the full spectrum, not necessarily in that order. Soap operas were not excluded, What kind of suds would Sartre, Beckett, Joyce, Ionesco or Billetdoux have written? What about Picasso as dress designer? Or Franco as director? The wine with brandy chasers was making us drunk. James Last and the smell of your perfume went to my head. We kissed.

Later in the afternoon you brought me to a small, intimate

mangerie in Place du Général Péret where your intimates were feasting on poissons and veg. I was introduced to the two Christines, Agnès, Laure and Emilie. The warm day mixed with fumes from the kitchen (not to speak of the alcohol!) made me light in the head – 'mal à cerveau', you said laughing – so we held hands and touched each other's legs. Do you remember me still?

The reason why I have not written to you before now is because my house in Dublin was burgled one Sunday night when I was asleep alone in my bed. All my valuables, including my precious address book, disappeared into the night. Last Friday my memory was returned to me by the police. It was found in the room of a man arrested for stealing a lorry-load of spirits. His name is O'Shea and he appeared in court today. He had a long history of aggravated burglary behind him. They found forty-odd address books and diaries in his wardrobe. I ask you! So, it's thanks to Mr O'Shea that I am writing to you now.

When we had finished our repast we walked up to Montmarte and Square Willette, looking at the artists, marvelling at the gaiety of nations. You called me your 'little gentil homme'; I returned the compliment with 'ma bonne femme'. Where is all this leading me? Well, that night it led us to bed. I'm afraid I dozed off on you – it was the walking and the drink that made me tired. I awoke at eleven next morning to find you gone. The cleaning lady said you worked in Centre National d'Art et de Culture Georges Pompidou, and that you usually returned at seven.

My darling Hélène, I'm afraid I cannot wait, my plane is leaving at five from Le Bourget, Apex non-refundable. I tried to call Pompidou. It's a huge place. I never did get your surname. Hélène who? Qui est-ce qui? They must have thought I was mad asking for a Hélène in a city of two million people. Your address went into O'Shea's book under 'H'. I suppose you don't live there anymore.

I'm writing just in case. Do you remember me, perchance? I love you.

> Votre ami,
> John O'Byrne

Dear Nigel,

When I told you last night that I was moving out, and going
down to Brighton today to find a new place to live, you only asked
whether that meant I wouldn't be back in time for dinner with
your guests. All very well, as reactions go, had ours been a
straight landlord/tenant relationship, with grunts in the morning,
nods last thing at night, brief encounters at the refrigerator door.
But for six months now we have been living in and out of one
another's life; I trotted on your heels as you walked round
Notting Hill in search of your perfect little Mews house. We
found it together, moved in together, chose new lights and hung
the hanging plants. I went with you to Italy, led you through the
Florence streets, ordered your food, picked out your gifts. I took
you home to meet the parents, and drove you three hours up to
Cardiff to be welcomed by your mother's chocolate roulade.
When your friends came to dinner, dreary accountants, hopeful
Sloanes, city slickers, I served the pasta and tried to hold my
tongue. You coped well with the lone radical feminist I brought to
the house, with pot-smoking intellectuals and Tom who pinned
up notices inviting us to Swapo meetings in Brixton Town Hall.
Anyway, I got fonder of your pin-striped profile than I ever
would have thought possible and you seemed rapidly to be falling
in love with me. Maybe I totally misread the situation: the special
warmth in your voice when I called you at the office, your looks
that lasted just a fraction longer, the thickening atmosphere when
it was time for you to go off to your narrow bed, and me to mine.
If I did, I wasn't the only one. Half our friends thought that we
were living together, not just sharing a house. You ate more
vegetables and less red meat, said that since I had moved in, your
commitment to your firm was weakening, dropped the token girl
friend summoned out for social occasions.

You still seemed to like me when I joined the ranks of the
unemployed. It was strange the way you never asked me how I
spent my days. I told you when I had interviews, and sometimes
let you in to the hundred plans I sat concocting while you read the
Financial Times. You got quite panicky when I talked about job
hunting in America, and when I mentioned Africa, said you
would come too. You kept repeating that you didn't see why I was
so desperate for work when I seemed so happy staying at home.

So marry me, I sometimes felt like screaming, if this is really how you think I should spend my life. It would spare me the embarrassment of paying a nominal rent, and seeing you flash a credit card whenever we went out. I tried to tell you that I felt like a kept woman, with the emphasis on the keeping since you never said a word or made a move to suggest you thought of me as anything more than a friend.

And then, about six weeks ago, things began to turn sour. I was out a lot, and so were you and we never asked each other a straight question about where we had been. You seemed to go calmly on with your stocking and broking while I got tenser and tenser, waiting for you to come home. When we hadn't had a 'meaningful conversation' for over two weeks, I decided to be very American about the whole affair and talk it over. You weren't much help, to say the least. I know I didn't really pick my time, bursting in that Sunday morning when you were barely dressed, and blurting out that we didn't seem to be getting on very well any more. You literally leapt two feet back, denied it vigorously, and went rushing off to buy Sunday papers while I was left to grind my teeth into rounds of toast. I did manage to tell you then that I had got my grant to take up a place at Sussex, and wanted to know what you thought of the idea. Did you really imagine I wanted your views on the course?

Is it possible to share lives for six months, and then to back out without so much as a goodbye? Perhaps, if you are as button-lipped and Public School as you have turned out to be. Don't you ever let rip with feelings, express an emotion, or do you really feel so little after five days a week of money-making on the stock exchange? Last night was my last ditch attempt, and now I'm tired of doing all the emotional spadework. I don't know whether there could have been anything between us. I would have found your fresh-faced looks and nursery manner hard. I'm not the blond, feather-haired, Laura Ashley type you go for. But I still think it's a miserable shame that we should have spent so much time and affection on our life together with nothing much to show. Oh, I know I will line up with Camilla, Clare and double-barrelled James in your address book. You may come down to Brighton, and I will be back to visit on weekends. We will talk about Nick and his pursuit of secretaries, about Justin and whether he has bought a house. You still won't ask me what it is that I am doing, and why. And I won't try to tell you. I feel you have slammed a door on what might have been a wider world, and you've shut me out there too. And that hurts.

D

Dear Eric,

I am leaving you, I want to be myself for one year or perhaps five. I want a sabbatical, after 30 years I deserve a sabbatical year off. I *would* like to come back!

I have enjoyed being a wife and mother, but after being a full-time mother the nest is empty, my role is over. I just cannot go back to being just a boring wife again, at least not just now. Our friends and dinner parties are boring or rather I am getting boring.

When we first married, it was lovely, you were my 'God', my mentor, I had been nowhere, done nothing. I was even frightened of the doorman at the Regent Palace Hotel in London, I remember wondering if he would let me in. But after 2 years I realized that you were not ambitious, never wanted much, would never go up the ladder, were just happy in a steady 9-5 routine life.

Giving birth to our daughter was lovely, that was a success. I felt so clever, we both felt good, and you were a wonderful father to her. She has proved that by marrying her father-image. Her husband is so like you, I do hope she does not outgrow him. But she no longer needs me. I must not interfere.

Giving birth to our son was a different matter – as you say he seemed a virgin birth. He takes after me 100%, all my faults exaggerated, also all my good points just a little larger than life. But he could have done with a stronger father, a mentor, someone to look up to, someone to admire and respect. I must go away and let him make his own mistakes.

Neither of them needs me now. I need to be needed, wanted, loved, cared for, listened to, caressed. I have found a lover, no not a toy boy, a man your age who without your advantages has made a real success of his life. He owns shops, businesses, has a big wad of money that I can waste. Morally I have never felt able to waste your money.

He treats me like a Queen. I want to have lots of champagne in the bath, let it spill over the glasses. Be wasteful. Rip expensive stockings.

I want to be noisy, shout, laugh loudly, sit in boxes at the theatre, two in a box for eight. Dance at expensive nightclubs, order rich dishes, taste them and not leave a clean plate. Even you knew I always wanted a power-drive automatic car, he lets me drive his. It's a company car, not important, not like ours were, Tin Gods to worship. He smashed up his car, our only worry was the tape of love songs in the car. Fortunately they were safe to play in another car. I want my lover to buy me chocolates from HARRODS. I want to choose them, watch them being wrapped and only eat a few. I want to buy all the magazines and papers and just glance at them and leave them untidy wherever I wish.

I just want to be a lady, a queen, a mistress for a few years.

No, it's not your fault, I have not been unhappy, but I just wish a slice of fantasy, before I take my next role as a Grandmother. That is if you let me come back after my sabbatical.

Your loving wife,
Pauline

My dear Hugh,

That's what you were once, a long time ago. A very long time
ago. I am trying to picture you now, staring at this envelope in
puzzlement, pushing your glasses back up to the top of your nose
and wrinkling your sandy brows. Only of course they won't be
sandy any more. I can't imagine the handwriting is remotely
familiar after all these years, and the postmark won't be much
help either. You'll have to look at the end of the letter to see who
it's from and even then I wonder, will you remember? It's a
common enough name.

We've just moved house and my youngest daughter Jenny has
been helping this week, washing china and sorting books. It was
the book-sorting that brought you back, because an old snapshot
of you fluttered out as she banged about with her duster, and she
pounced on it with great curiosity. Jenny always wants to know
everything about everybody. So I say, 'A man I used to know at
university'. And Jenny says, 'Oh Mum, was it serious? I mean a
real Affair?' By which I understand her to be asking me if you and
I were lovers, since that is what she would expect in today's
world. But I choose to answer her literally and say, 'Oh no my
love. Whatever it was it wasn't serious. It was the funniest, most
light-hearted bit of my whole life!' Jenny stares, and I beam back,
feel remembered laughter bubbling up inside me and try to tell
her what it was like when we were young.

It was an odd time wasn't it? The war was well and truly over
but we were still in that period when lots of students were
ex-Servicemen. As you were. Many of the men were in their mid
and late twenties, mature, self-confident, worldly-wise. Some of
them had killed men in battle. You had. Very dazzling for girls
straight from school, some still in ankle socks, few wearing
make-up, all of us green as the spring grass. No wonder we fell in
love all over the place.

Jenny says, 'He's not exactly handsome is he?' And I agree; but
remember with affection square, competent scrubbed hands,
forever moving vigorously to illustrate whatever story you were
telling, a long, thin face vivid in a group round a table, grinning a
warm welcome to me across a crowded refectory. How quickly it
came about that the day didn't get started properly until I saw
your immensely tall, stringy figure striding along College Street;

you wore an army greatcoat, and the back of your neck went unfashionably red in the sun, and when I ran to meet you, you swung me up off my feet. We met at the beginning of my finals year, and we parted at the end of it.

And of course Jenny asks, 'What happened?' and I stare at her, and shake my head, and have no answer, because I have never really understood what happened. So I'm writing to ask you after more than thirty years, what did happen? The summer term was a whirl of exams, succeeded by end-of-term dances, graduations and farewells, job-hunting and interviews, and a great deal of emotion. We walked and talked and clung, just managed not to sleep together and complained bitterly of the fate that had come up with a lectureship for you some three hundred miles away while I felt duty-bound to look for something nearer home and my solitary mother. We parted at the station, tears from me and passionate avowals from you; and there were letters for a while, loving but increasingly vague on your part, and then they petered out, and that was that.

So why am I writing to you now? Perhaps it's because I'm old enough to. I'm not really into raking up the past or mooning over lost loves you know, but I am increasingly anxious in middle age to see myself as honestly as I can, yet I cannot for the life of me see that twenty-year-old self at all clearly. Was I submissive, naive, prudish, entertaining or a dead bore? And I suppose more than anything else I would like to know whether I was of value to you. You certainly made me feel so for a time, but then you chose to disappear from my life so it was not possible to believe it any more. I do know I was one in a long series of young women. I remember you assuring me gravely that you could provide first-class references from previous employers, which seemed marvellously witty at the time when I was busy saying 'No' to staying the night. Was I the first to say 'No'? Would things have been different if I hadn't?

I fell in love again of course, more than once. Some were cleverer than you, some were more charming, almost all of them were better-looking. Some I tired of and one I married. But none of them were quite as kind and funny. (Jenny thinks these requisites very strange; she likes men to be tall, dark and handsome and intellectually brilliant.) I've been considering my three daughters and Mike, my son, and wonder what they'd have been like if you had fathered them. They wouldn't have been so beautiful but I'm absolutely sure they'd have had more fun.

How useful it is that I've taught and you've written two or three language textbooks, so I can write to you c/o your publisher. You'll realize I haven't given you my address. I thought I might add it now, at the end, but I shan't after all. Cold feet if you like, or common sense; you choose.

With a little love, still,
Rosemary

Dear Michael,

If only, just two short words, yet they can mean so much. It seems like yesterday when we parted, though it's been six years. Six years of experiencing and learning but not one day has passed by without you being in my thoughts and in my heart. If only we knew then what we know now. If only we had met when we were a little older and wiser, when our love would have been more mature and then circumstances would not have come between us, we would not have allowed them to. It seems so pointless you living in Australia and me in England, but then circumstances played a large part in that again. I remember back in 1973 when we boarded that ocean liner that was going to take us to the other side of the world, we were full of enthusiasm and excited anticipation of what lay in front of us and for six years life was so full. How could we forget touring Aussie in a $600 station wagon, through territory that did not have bitumen roads, what a harrowing yet interesting trip that was, through the red mountain ranges of the Simpson Desert to Alice Springs, from the centre of Australia to the tropical, lush vegetation of the Barrier Reef Islands. And you were always there, and so was I. To comfort each other and to laugh together and cry together. And do you remember when we landed in Bali, the first sector on our trip back to England through the Middle East and South East Asia, feeling sheer wonderment at that beautiful island, the smell of incense everywhere, the priests sitting by the side of the road chanting their religious songs, the serene women walking about with things on their heads, and staying in bamboo huts and eating fried rice that had been cooked in the tiniest kitchens imaginable. I wonder what would have happened if we had not decided to return to Australia. I wonder what would have happened if you had not met that musician and joined his band, if I had not met that charming chap who was so concerned to give me a good time and take my mind away from the suddenly terrible and frightening realization that we were having more and more difficulty communicating. It was such a vicious circle wasn't it, you pursuing a dream that you'd had since childhood took so much of your time and resulted in us seeing each other only about two evenings a week. We were both too young to see the pitfalls, weren't we, we had come to take each other for granted, hadn't

27

we? We'd been so very close, I suppose we thought we'd always be there for each other. Now we must know from sheer experience that it can be so destructive to take such a beautiful love for granted.

Eventually you became a recognized musician, you had such talent, and I, after a string of affairs, fell in love with that charming chap who I met to start with. Now I know that there are many different kinds of love, many different levels of intensity, but the kind of love I had for you and still do is the enduring kind that lasts a lifetime and never dies. It was based on a very deep friendship, on mutual respect and admiration, on caring for each other when the other was ill. For years your face haunted me, your kind beautiful eyes, whenever I woke up you were right there in front of me. You have never really left me. When we parted the pain of losing you was too intense for me even to be able to cry for three years. That other chap I never really missed, it was a superficial love, the kind that flickers like a candle then the flame goes out. It would never have withstood the reality of day-to-day life. But we had far more going for us than anyone I know. We shared innermost thoughts, I knew I could tell you anything and that you would never use anything against me, I knew I could trust you totally, you were without doubt the most sensitive person I have ever known apart from my mother. She died a few months ago. You were always so gentle with her, as you were with everyone. It made me re-evaluate my life when they thought I had cancer last year. I thought about life and what it represents to me now, and how my values have changed vastly, how I used to think success was so important or material possessions or travelling and enjoying life to the full. But I realize now that the most important thing of all, that had any sort of meaning for me whatsoever, was loving you. What we shared I will never forget, not until my dying day. Somebody said to me the other day that there is not much that money cannot buy, including health and I replied that there is one thing that goes beyond all that and that is true love. My darling, you are priceless. The most important thing to me now is that you are happy whatever it may take. I know you have married again. I know too through reliable sources that you do not love her as you still love me, that I too am special to you as you are to me, that you married her because you cared for her and didn't want to be alone anymore. I left it up to you to contact me if you needed to because I didn't want to pressurize you in any way, how could I have known you were doing the same thing?

How can I ever forget our wedding day, a blissfully sunny day in June. You looked so handsome in a tailor-fit three-piece suit, and I was dressed in a beautiful Edwardian wedding gown, and when the wedding car arrived we put our friends in it while we walked gaily hand in hand to the Registry Office and much, much later when we were on our own in a boat rowing along the Serpentine in Hyde Park, people were smiling and wishing us luck and throwing us flowers in the boat. We talked about our dreams, about our future, about the two children we would have, the house with the roses in the front garden, how we would be together for always. If only –

Love,
Nicky

(E. J. Wilson)

Dear Ange,

Thanks for your letter. I must say it precipitated quite a debate between Hazel and myself. Rather than resign myself to the 'Sigh! What can we do at this distance?' approach, I've decided to write an open letter that comes full of sisterly love but nevertheless may appear a little strong.

Angie, my love, you are in danger. The danger is not of being alone. It is far worse. There has seeped into your everyday life, and the baggage of philosophy that fashions your attitudes, a terrible fatalism of 'Ho hum, I'm never going to be happy – still you can't have everything can you?' Do you even realize how much like Mum that sounds? But Mum is speaking after 30 years of a heart-breakingly vacuous marriage. What's your excuse? None that I can accept. By allowing your present situation to drag on as you are, putting yourself out into no-man's land, you could be waiting by the window and intoning Joni Mitchell songs for the next 20 years if you don't watch out.

You probably think I'm trying to twist your arm so that you'll go ahead with the wedding. It's not true. This terrible, meandering, wistful state of non-events must be terminated and quickly. You must decide something. If you can't let Bobby go, then marry him and spend the rest of your life making sure it works. If it feels so wrong then end it once, finally and for all time with him. No reunions, no last-chance weekends in the Lakes, no birthday cards, no just-good-friends ambiguities. Finish it – see him again in three years when you feel better and perhaps then you'll be friends.

It is true that the situation you find yourself in offers a sort of security – it obviates the need for decision. All the factors (the personalities, the pressures) are familiar. However, you must surely see that the security it offers is a limited and totally artificial one. You have placed yourself in suspended animation frozen in space if not in time – which is inexorably moving on. To say you are worried about finishing with Bobby because of the isolation on the other side is just no argument. You are good with people, make friends easily, popular quickly, intelligent, humorous and pretty as a picture. All the fundamental ingredients for your happiness exist already within you. These are the best years of your life and what are you doing with them?

I don't want to hear any more about fate. The fate that's rapidly overtaking you is one you have now brought upon your own head. How long do you intend languishing in your own misery, shrugging your shoulders, reading of the broken people in the world of Scott Fitzgerald? Shake yourself out of this, Angie, for all our sakes. No one else can do it. Summon up all the strength you've ever had and throw it all into one final, irrevocable decision: Go or no-go, Bobby or freedom, marriage or break-up. Don't wait for dreamy salvation. Act now.

I hope I've made my point. I don't want you to feel guilty on account of the rest of the family. However, if you don't do something positive and final you are going to sink into a role that marks you out forever as 'Poor Ange'. Don't worry, we'll support you and love you just the same – whatever you decide. Your future can be saved if you will only act. Write and tell me you've done it.

All my love,
Sister Suze

(Suzy Epstein)

My dearest Roy,

Well I am writing this letter to you after what seems to have been one of the longest years in my life. It is nearly a year to the day since you called at my mother's house on my birthday with a settlement cheque and a card, took me out for a pub lunch and then walked out of my life.

In three weeks' time we will have been married for 20 years and where did all those years go? So many memories and so many goodbyes. I never realized just how many times in those 20 years I would kiss you goodbye, sometimes for weeks but more often than not for months at a time. Yes, being married to a soldier isn't the easiest kind of marriage, but it is certainly different!!

Life was never dull, only on occasions very lonely especially when you were gone on a long posting and then everything became a game of crossing off the days on the calendar until you would be home. The postman must have wondered what two people had so much to write about – little did he know that, on occasions, the letter inside the envelope just had scribbled across the page LOVE AND MISS YOU because at the time you were in Northern Ireland and patrolling the streets and just didn't have time to write. Then there were the postcards from what looked like exotic places, well for the tourists maybe, but not for the soldiers. I still have the photograph of the scrubbed-out cow-shed that you lived in and called 'home' for a while in South America during a six-month tour.

Well the years went by and we continued to move house. Germany, Gibraltar, Berlin to name but a few of the more exotic parts of the world that I managed to see with you, but numerous others which you visited alone and which are recorded somewhere amongst the many photo albums now locked away.

So here we are 20 years on, each of us with our memories some happy and many sad. Life will never be the same again, I still cross off the days on the calendar, the postman still calls, but today there are no exotic postcards, no love letters from faraway places, just an emptiness that feels like it will go on forever. I hope you will forgive me for writing and encroaching on your new life, but I couldn't let the day go by without telling you how much you are still missed.

Happy anniversary.
Love,
Carol

(Mrs Carol Ann Scott)

Hi Sally,

Let's forget the formalities and get straight to the point.

WHY DID YOU RUN OFF WITH MY HUSBAND? Of all the dirty tricks you've played, I'd never have thought you were capable of doing this to me, your best friend (presently ex-best friend).

Never mind though, I'm being sensible and grown up about it and I'm consoled with the fact that you and my husband probably suit each other perfectly. HE'S A FAT SLOB AND I WOULD HAVE DIVORCED HIM IF HE'D STAYED! But you, just how could you do it to me? How could you tell me so many lies? You'd better stay away from me for the next fifty years because I'm feeling like the colour of my ink – DANGEROUS!!

I suppose you'll try and tell me you did it for love, yet I can't believe you'd love my old hubby who picks his nose in public and who's worn dentures for the last thirty years. Although, give him credit where it's due (and that's in very few places), HE IS LOADED! If you behave yourself you might get a pair of earrings every Christmas.

Well, I must fly, I've got a dinner date with Andrew Brooks (you know, tall and very handsome, who turned you down at our last party).

Good luck (because you'll need it),
Sarah

(Sarah Jones)

Dear Jack,

Well now, Jack, I suppose you're wondering why I haven't
been to see you yet. To tell you the truth, my nerves couldn't
stand it. I might slap you around the head with my social security
book or something.

God, Jack, if you could see us now, me and the girls, honest,
jumble-sale clothes, cardboard in our shoes and a staple diet of
beans on toast. Do you know, Jack, if I have to eat beans on toast
once more I'll burn down the factory that makes them.

I bet you get fed better there in Walton than we do. I bet you
don't get beans on toast every other day. Our Mandy says that's
the reason her bra's not filled as well as it should be, she says you
can't fill a 34B on beans on toast.

That damp patch on the ceiling's getting worse, there's nearly
as much pond life up there as on the banks of the Mersey. I'm
thinking of asking for a government grant to turn it into a nature
reserve! The backyard keeps getting flooded, we can't go to the
lavvi without our wellies. There's no chance of me being mistaken
for Bo Derek, not in your dad's old dressing-gown and black
wellies!

Oh Jack, I've had enough, I have honest. What with you taking
that stocking off your head in the bank to blow your nose, and
them getting it on the video camera! God Jack, we're a laughing
stock around here, there's copies of that blasted video on the
market, it's selling more than *Educating Rita*.

'How's your Jack's cold?' that's what they're all asking. Mandy
came home from school crying her eyes out, because the kids
keep giving her packets of Kleenex 'to send to your old man in
Walton'. They're calling you Vick now instead of Jack!

Your ma sends her regards. She says if they're ever daft enough
to let you out, you're to go straight to Pier Head and jump in.
You've let the family down, Jack. You wouldn't have caught your
dad in Barclays with a inhaler up his nose.

It's all right for you in there you know, Jack; me and the girls
have got to live around here. Try holding your head up when
every other person you meet is offering you their free sample of
Day Nurse that came in the post.

Speaking of post, I'd better get a move on or I'll miss the 3
o'clock pick up.

I would send you all my love, but I haven't got the energy, there's 4p off beans down the market so I'd better get down there and get a supply in.

Tara Jack,
Lynn

(Lynn Johnson)

Dearest Amir,

Now, after leaving you at Heathrow and returning to what was our home together for fourteen years, all is still. Pregnant with silence, my thoughts surround me.

I feel as if my world has been inverted. Here am I, in what is now your house, although you are living and working abroad most of the time.

Our bond, however, is constant. Our son. To you, as an Arab, he is like a god. No daughter could have given you the same pride. You were even proud when you used to recount to people that our other premature son, who died after only two hours, was also a boy. We were mortified by his death, but your male ego remained in your idea that virility produced yet another son!

We have technically been apart for more than four years now. We have experienced the finality of divorce. Was I too hasty to divorce you? What may be unreasonable behaviour to one nationality, may be quite normal behavour to another. Shall we ever know?

For me, though, having lived with you for fourteen years, thinking, as you had told me, that you were a lapsed Roman Catholic and half Armenian, to later find out you were a Shia Moslem and had no Armenian connections, was a big shock.

We had lived through so many years of difficulties. Your student years when I worked to help to support you when your Embassy stopped your grant. Those were frugal years, spent in an attic room in a multi-nationality house. Do you remember the smell of garlic cooking in the Turk's room? Also the huge Maltese lady standing outside the house watching her friends, the owners, leave to go on holiday, as she waved them off with a long french loaf?

What about the time I put your hair in rollers, just for fun? How surprised that English student looked when he knocked on our door. You answered and stood talking to him, fogetting all about the rollers and pink hair net. Those were the days when 'drag' was not the 'in' thing! No wonder he was amazed. How we laughed afterwards.

Eventually you qualified. We felt so optimistic. However, being a foreigner then, it was not easy for you to find a job. Little by little we built up our lives. We went abroad with our baby son, for you to work in the torrid heat of the desert.

Your temper though did not always endear you to your employers. You lost seven jobs. I hate lying, but you will also remember how my father called one day and I told him you were working on a design at home. He never approved of our marriage, and I did not want to see him feel hurt that you were unemployed.

Life was not easy, but I loved you with such intensity and was prepared for almost anything...Now, I remember with horror how your brother came to visit you in England. It was Christmas 1980. You did not return. You were held up abroad, fighting a court case against unfair dismissal. Once again you were unemployed.

You had never let me meet your family, always going to meet them alone. I never understood why. Gradually the reason dawned. Your brother, who was a very simple person, had no idea of what you had told me over the years. As I talked to him I discovered that you were not half Armenian as you had told me, nor had you a brother in Russia who was a deserter. In fact he did not even exist anywhere! So it went on.

As a previous market research investigator, I warmed to my subject. I discovered, and saw documentary proof, that you had not told me the truth about yourself. Suddenly, I did not seem to know the man I thought to be my husband. Suddenly you were a stranger.

I telephoned you to say that I was going to divorce you. I felt so deeply hurt. Hurt that you had lied to me. Why darling? When we met, you were beside yourself with worry because you had made a fifteen-year-old girl pregnant. I stood by you, found a helpful lawyer, you did not even have to go to court. I even sent the maintenance money each month,because you told me it hurt you to remember. I with my mistaken Anglo-Saxon outlook, thought you would always remember this, and that it would help us to build a good marriage.

My life suddenly seemed shattered, my confidence in you dissolved like a mirage.

Four years, and much trauma, has elapsed since then. I could not find a job in England. In desperation I went to France where I found work. France saved me. You stopped our son visiting me, although you did not openly admit it. You wanted to own him.

Eventually fate took a hand. I found a job in England, for

which I was interviewed in France. We were then brought together by an unexpected meeting. You seemed so much more open and relaxed. Time had changed you. We ate at an hotel near Heathrow, as the winter's worst blizzard raged outside, and your plane was cancelled due to a sandstorm in Cairo! I have since blessed that sandstorm.

We arranged to meet again on your next trip to England. We kept writing to each other. How wonderful it was in May when we spent the entire ten days together. Neither of us was emotionally committed to anyone else. Our new relationship started to blossom. Time had healed many of the wounds.

Thank you for the lovely holiday you gave us in North Africa this summer. It was a time for our now teenage son to spend an intensive two weeks with me.

You then returned again in July, and we realized that we would like to build a new future together. You have met others in these intervening years, but as you say 'nobody understands me as you do'.

Perhaps we have disproved, or may disprove in the future, who knows, Kipling's theory that 'East is East, and West is West, and never the twain shall meet.'

Now I am waiting for the New Year when you return once again. Another Heathrow rendezvous!

I send you my love with growing anticipation of a beautiful future.

> With love and happy memories,
> Anne

Dearest darling,

I've just got your dear call (d'you know, this one was number 435!) and you've urged me to answer to your most important question, but I don't know how to begin with.

I'm sitting in my lounge, surrounded by all the bookshelves, radio and telly, the phone by my side. My canary's cage is placed near the window, in midst of flowers and plants. I'm listening to a flute concert by Mozart. All very peaceful, in fact. It's slightly raining outside, your roses are in a vase on my table. They look tired, worn out and remind me how transient and fragile life is. Near them there's the horsechestnut found on our last walk together in your beloved country. It says, autumn has come, nature is preparing for the harvest, will fall asleep soon and relax under snowflakes dreaming of a new spring, our next and first spring together, you've said. The canary is sleeping. Let's hope he'll live to see next spring... Life is transient and passes fast indeed. People and things alter continuously, growing or decaying or both... (Oh dearest, I imagine your beloved face now, could I hold your hand now, at least!) However, we've reached the second half (half??) of our life, you say, and we'd consider what to do with the remaining part of it...

Your dear thoughts have always helped me, darling, they encourage me, and our relationship has revealed much about my inner self, in fact, hidden and oppressed wants and needs that are essential and long for fulfilment. In those bygone years, when I'd been nursing my deadsick husband did I act out of compulsion and a mixture of love and pity but in a way I was dying inside, always denying myself, considering only him and his wishes. (You've said, it wasn't until we met first that you've seen what you'd been lacking and in a way had always been longing for in your own marriage, darling, haven't you?)

Oh dearest, never will I forget those first hours! I'd come to Exeter to see an old schoolfriend of mine, to forget about the dreadful end of my marriage and we were waiting for a guided tour through the town. When you turned up and we took you for the guide and you said you were not but suggested to come with us, oh dear, I felt as if I'd known you always, just met an old friend. We'd fallen for each other at first sight. Hadn't I taken the photograph of us three, never would we have seen again! D'you remember, when you told me you were married, how fast I parted refusing to have another drink with you after my schoolfriend had left us to do some shopping? I didn't even give you the ring you'd asked for before I left England. When I sent the photograph to you and to my schoolfriend I didn't expect more than a greeting card, but you started writing and phoning, asked me to come again and so long did you insist till I came back a year later just to tell you how impossible things were. Yes, you said, you agreed in everything with me till I didn't know what else to say... That first night, when we stayed together, too shy to touch each other, like two children, just looking at each other, when we climbed out the ground-floor window, walked around hand in hand looking in each other's eyes (I love your smiling face) telling each other so many things! How many times did we see one another since then? I've been torturing myself about many things ever since, but couldn't help loving you more and more (and you did as well I suppose!) Each time when we met for some days or just for hours, did I say to myself, that's the last time now, never shall I come again, that's our last walk together, our last stay, our last night, oh darling, you shouldn't have taken me to your sister's house, you shouldn't have asked me that question. Time passes, life passes, you said, I'll divorce my wife I want to live with you, you've said, next spring will be our spring, our first one and others will follow and never shall we part again. There's no other alternative, you said, beloved soulmate. I look at your roses. At the horsechestnut, at my sleeping canary. Life is transient, life is fragile, am I right? And we're as well dearest. I can't, I can't break another's happiness just because of selfishness. Haven't you said, in a way do you still love your wife? And doesn't she love you even if you don't get along together as well as you'd want?

Hadn't you asked me that question, that final question, I wouldn't have found the power to part from you, but I can't, I simply can't build up my luck on another's misfortune, dearest. I'd be grateful you'd asked me that, in fact, it's brought me back to reality back to my better self. Forgive me please, I can't give you another answer, and I do hope you'll agree with me (not just now but at a later date), as you agreed when we'd stayed together for the first time...

God bless you both.

(And please, forgive my many mistakes, I know, my English is still not very good, even after so much training, how often did you laugh at my odd mistakes! Am I right? I'm not going to say goodbye, I say good night.)

J. T. Brix

Dear Lisa,

You are reading between the lines again and this time I'll admit
that you are right. Yes, it's about Edward. It won't change
anything writing it all down, but it might help. You see he lied to
me, and I find it so hard to forgive. You will be wondering how I
could be so secretive but I simply couldn't make myself tell the
whole sordid story. Everybody though he was so marvellous such
a success, so honest and decent, that sometimes it seems
impossible to believe it was all an act. Maybe too I have the faint
hope that you will find a flaw in my story, or something that I
have missed. If only you could. Can you remember how excited I
was before I left for Paris. After all we hadn't met for a year and
although phone calls and letters are a help they are poor
substitutes. It was pure joy to see him again and I suppose looking
back I was blind not to see a change in him but he looked so fit
and happy. The next two days were wonderful. Don't ask me
where we went or what we did, but it was all that I thought it
would be. Then it began to fall apart. At dinner on the second
night he became very quiet and when I remarked about it he told
me he had been troubled by a sharp chest pain. That worried me,
but as he was his normal self again in a few minutes I didn't say
too much about it. He mentioned some phone calls and letters he
had to attend to so I was left on my own afterwards – I felt quite
piqued, but I wasn't alarmed. It was about 3 a.m. when the phone
rang. He was speaking from the reception desk. He'd felt ill again
and called the hotel doctor who insisted that he go into hospital.
That was so like him. Even at a time like that he was in full
control. I was at the hospital at 8 a.m. and he was awake and out
of pain, but the doctors told me quite bluntly he had only a few
hours to live. It was so incredible that I wondered if we were
speaking about the same person. Edward knew, because he told
me where to find the address of his attorney who would deal with
everything. Before I fianlly accepted what was happening I asked
him if I could go back with him by private plane and I was hurt by
his explosive 'no'.

I didn't have time to analyse his reaction but I was left with a
feeling of disquiet. He died at midday. I eventually got round to
phoning his attorney who sounded exactly like an American actor
playing the part of an attorney – brash and tough. To be fair he

was also efficient. That, I thought, was that. When the phone rang during the night I thought he was back with more questions, but a soft young voice said, 'This is Jenny,' I said, 'Who?' She repeated her name and added that she was Edward's daughter! I answered that he didn't have a daughter, only a son who was 24 years old. We batted this back and forward a few times before I managed to think up a couple of questions like what was her age and her mother's name. She was 14 years old and her mother's name was correct. How had she managed to contact me? The attorney had called her brother who was on holiday in some inaccessible place so she had decided to act on her own. It is rather difficult to describe how I felt after I put the phone down. I didn't believe her, partly because she has been born four years after Edward's divorce, but also because vague stories went through my mind about people claiming kinship whenever a wealthy person does. When the attorney rang later to confirm arrangements I told him about the girl and immediately I sensed a wariness in his voice. He said he believed there was a daughter and when I asked if she was Edward's real daughter he said, 'Well Edward pays for her upkeep.' This is when I really needed someone to talk to, a friend who was not involved and who could give an impartial opinion. You see I knew so much about his son, that he was given custody of him when he was 11 years old, and how he had just graduated as a civil engineer. So many stories which built up a picture of a good father/son relationship. If only I hadn't been so dazzled by his personality I might have been quicker to pick out details which didn't fit. It was long after I was back home that I finally gave up trying to keep my dream. It was the difference in the dates that did it. First, he said his divorce was in 1966 which would make his son 7 years old not 11 when he was given custody of him. Second, the girl was born 4 years after the date of divorce yet she carries his name, and he pays maintenance. So reluctantly I came to the conclusion that he had changed the date of his divorce, probably to keep up his image of the Knight in Shining Armour, the Winner. Everybody had to be second to him. I wonder if his wife really was an alcoholic, after all she was allowed to keep the baby. Yet all my sympathy must go to that young girl, whose father denied her existence. How could I have been so blind?

I am sorry to trouble you with my problems, but you have been wondering why I didn't write more often, and anyway it will be good to have your views on all this. At least I can depend on you to give me an honest opinion.

Love,
Anna

(Anna Hurst)

RELATIVELY SPEAKING

Dear Daddy,

I've been looking at that family photograph again – the one taken almost a year ago. There we all are – the round dozen of us – at the hotel on John's wedding day. Of all the photographs, it's the one I cherish most.

The tell-tale Christmas tree in the background, hung with tinsel and shiny glass balls, proclaims it's the 'festive season' – the 15th December, to be exact. The buttonholes, the various colourful outfits, the three handsome young men, in identical white shirts, black jackets and pin-striped trousers, confirm the occasion is a wedding.

In actual fact, it was the wedding of your first son. After 'giving away' seven daughters, I think you were relieved not to have to do any more 'aisle trotting', weren't you? And no more speeches! You raised a laugh on the last occasion when you said – from the heart – 'Thank God it's the last time I'll have to go through this palaver. It's all boys from now on!'

This was the photograph you insisted on being taken, no matter what. You were adamant about it, 'Come on, you never know when we will all be together again!' Husbands were excluded, children extricated from their mothers' arms, the boys prised away from the bar! The foyer was briefly taken over by the Harron clan – a few flashes, and that was it! The whole family together, mother, father, seven daughters, three sons – after all those years. We attracted quite a bit of attention, although that wasn't the intention.

It was the first time we had all managed to be together, in one place, without a missing member, for fifteen years! We almost made it, do you remember, when Anne was married, only Serena was in India. People might ask, why didn't we get around to it before? Well, the trouble was, with such a brood, the fledglings had already started to leave the nest, while the other eggs were still hatching. In short, the birds had flown – to build their own nests! You know what I mean!

It's a lovely photograph, isn't it? You, greying, but still handsome and upright, and so proud. Mammy, on the other side, gentle, smiling, amazingly slim, to be the mother of ten. We seven 'girls', sandwiched between the two of you, in our best regalia. I remember the jockeying for position, so as not to 'clash' with each other in the colour photo. Jane's shocking pink was to blame! The boys, although younger, are all taller than we are, so we made them crouch in front of us! They grumbled a bit at the time but, in the photo, their smiles are as wide as all the others. Everyone remarks what a good-looking family we are – there can't be many men with such a fine bunch, even if I say so myself!

And after the photos – the fun and the games, the music and the dancing. You were the life and soul of the party as usual. I remember you, dancing first with your new daughter-in-law, then your daughters, whirling us around the floor, as you whistled in time to the music. Your great good humour, your liveliness, your infectious *joie de vivre*, united the two families, as the priest had earlier united the young couple.

And then, to cheers and clapping, which embarrassed her greatly, you dragged Mammy on to the floor for a waltz. Once again, you were insistent – you wouldn't take 'no' for an answer. We knew she hated dancing as much as you loved it, if only because of her extreme shyness and self-consciousness. We knew we were witnessing something unique at that moment – our mother and father, dancing together for the first time in public. She was blushing like a schoolgirl, you were enjoying the limelight!

Back home after the reception, do you remember getting out that little black volume – the poems of Robert Burns? We knew what we were in for! In your best Scottish accent,

> Wee cowerin', sleeked, timorous beastie,
> Oh what a panic's in thy breastie . . .

and

My love is like a red, red rose...

and

> Oh wad the Lord the gift did gie us
> To see ourselves as others see us...

I'm sorry I ragged you about him, saying he had been a bit of a lad – *you* would have none of it! And honestly Daddy, the yawns were because we were so tired after the 'hooley'! It's funny really, that an Irish working man should be so fond of the works of a Scottish poet. Callouses on the hands, but not on the heart, that was you.

After the wedding... the wake. Your leaving was so sudden, so unexpected. God knows shy He snatched away your retirement years after a lifetime of hard work... the labour of love. Mammy especially misses you. She telephoned today with news of her twelfth grandchild, James's son. You know already don't you? Andrew, they're calling him. Andrew Harron, your name. I know you'll be pleased.

Thank you for all the love and the happy memories. Thank you for this photograph – look over my shoulder one last time before I put it away. Rest in peace, dear, dear Daddy.

Your ever loving daughter,
Jane xxx

My dearest,

You know how I have always loved to write letters. While I write you are completely mine, even if not for long. And letters are almost always connected with memories. And memories somehow purify and brighten the past, even if in it there was much that was dark and painful.

While I write these lines I find myself in childhood, which for me passed under the portrait of a bright-eyed man, full of youth and affection. David. My father. Englishman. Journalist. Brilliant. A lover of women. Generous and reckless. An enormous capacity to work and to play.

Of course all that I know of you is what I've heard from my mother, who remembers you as an angel who flew into cold and hungry post-war Moscow. Were you really like that? Or were you an ideal she needed in order to survive those terrible years when her friends disappeared one by one into the Siberian camps? Or perhaps you were my fantasy? I don't know. To tell you the truth I didn't really want to ever see you. For me you were an idea, not a real person. But still I felt absolutely clearly your presence somewhere, in an unknown world, that gave me a feeling of having been chosen. Thanks to you I wasn't like everybody else.

Once a visiting sportsman brought us a letter. In honour of such an event we put out on the table the heavy silver bowl filled with fruit. After the sportsman's visit the bowl stayed on the table a long time, almost a month. My mother didn't have the strength to put it away. Somehow she had just wilted. Literally in a couple of hours the young Moscow beauty had turned into a grey-haired woman, with sallow skin and two deep, bitter lines on each side of her mouth. From that time on I never liked young sportsmen.

I never told you about that when we at last met a quarter of a century later. Why? Maybe because I didn't want to open old wounds. That letter had been the end of all my mother's hopes. The most important thing had been to live, grow old and die with you.

You told me that there had not been a single day in all those years that you didn't remember us, suffer for us. But I don't believe you, I just don't believe you. I know that ten years is a long time. That you could meet another woman and fall in love. But how could you – with your talent, sincerity and taste – write such a banal, cowardly letter, a lie from beginning to end? Your fatal illness, and some nurse who had saved you and whom you had to marry out of gratitude. How could you respond to love and hope with something of such dreadful taste, that calm, calculating letter, with its careful doses of sentimentality and correctness, like a bad Victorian novel? With that letter you began the destruction of the image I had of you. You killed yourself in me. And that murder I cannot forgive.

My dearest, my beloved father. Do you remember how you read your book to me in English, and then translated it into Russian, your book about Dante's wife, who hated Beatrice and in her hatred tried to become better, more intelligent, more human that Beatrice. She struggled with a beautiful vision and won herself a new humanity.

In those brief hours you truly were the person under whose portrait I had passed my childhood. But then I heard the uncertain steps on the stairs, a bottle clinked in the next room as your wife poured herself another gin. You began to fuss around, put away the papers and files, trying to hide your fright. The magic passed. Once again I saw before me a man no longer young who unlike his heroine had crippled himself and all those around him.

You introduced me to your former wives, including Lola with whom you still lived. And from your conversations I put it all together, I understood the letter which had destroyed my mother. You couldn't and didn't want to hide anything. I was happy that you were so open with me. I liked to be the witness of your romantic adventures. In your stories all your women were so wonderful, even Lola. You shone in my hungry attention. Probably all your life you had hoped that a woman would appear who would take you as you were, not a patchwork of fantasies and hopes. And that woman, the last woman in your life, would be me, a daughter, a listener, a companion.

My darling, believe me, I really did suffer over your bitter failures. And I still marvel at your toughness, how you got back up again and again. But don't judge me – I'm not the woman who can forgive everything. You never managed to understand the simple truth: 'We are responsible for those who trust us and rely on us.' And we all trusted you totally and unconditionally. And for that we are all paying. Your women are left alone forever –

after you no one could fill their hearts. Somewhere in Italy Lola is drinking herself to death. And me . . . well, we'll see.

My dearest, my beloved, my unhappy father. I know that all your life you felt guilty before us all. You were exhausted by the burden, tired of us. But then, with a final burst of energy, you decided to return to your past, to find your Moscow family.

How we tortured you those five days you were in Moscow. We dragged you around the theatres, we kept you up all night, we overwhelmed you with endless questions. We tried to live 25 years in five days. Then you invited me to England. And immediately, from the first day, I became a witness to the reckoning that life had made with you. A drunken woman poured on to you all the hatred and hurt that was your life together. And you replied with bitter, hateful words. Once, during yet another fight, you literally shoved me into the car. A few minutes later we were in some big shop. You tore the things off the hangers and threw them at me. You looked as if you were going to buy everything in the shop. This was your despairing attempt to show Lola that you had someone to care about, somebody to love in this world. I could feel so keenly what was happening to you. And at that moment a very clear and simple thought came into my mind: you had searched for me and my mother just so you could show Lola that somewhere someone was still waiting for you, that somewhere someone loved you.

My dearest, it is five years since you died. Was it the trip to Moscow that did it? You died in the night. Quietly. A heart attack. You didn't call Lola, ask her to call a doctor. She found you dead. In the morning.

A day doesn't go by that I don't think of you. I hear your voice, stroke your soft, almost childlike cheeks, see myself in your eyes. I love you very much. And I hate you. I must tell you that – I've carried it in me far too long. And if somewhere you hear me, then forgive me. And be happy for me. If it hadn't been for my trip to England I wouldn't have met my husband. And there wouldn't have been another little person to appear on this earth to carry on.

Your daughter,
Helen Fortescue

Dear Nancy,

At last I feel able to sort out my emotions and write this letter.
More to the point it is three in the morning and I've a large
whisky in front of me which always reminds me of our midnight
discussions.

The trouble is where to start? Three years ago you said I
couldn't thank you personally for your gift and I was never to
refer to that conversation again. All right, I haven't mentioned it,
I'm just writing about it.

I've been trying to analyse our relationship since your death
and concluded because it didn't follow the usual pattern of two
single women exploring their freedom is exactly why it worked.
What good company you were in my early unsettled days and not
a bit like Mum – you'd never think you were sisters. Two giggly
women on the rampage with a difference of 30 years and £300,000
between them. I loved staying at Farhills Manor with its luxury of
isolation, and envied the girls their childhood exploring the fields
and gardens, playing in the attic rooms. Even more, having their
own bedrooms with the ultimate luxury to me – their own
bathrooms. I often think back to when we played there as kids
and can still remember how much more freedom we had with you
compared to my over-strict Mother. Those lovely midnight feasts
we had when I was allowed to snuggle up to you in bed before
Uncle John shouted at me. You were much plumper then and
lovely and soft – you used to let me have a taste of your whisky if I
promised not to tell. The sprawling kitchen with its big wooden
table where we exchanged recipes when I was married, tears when
Alan left, and giggles when we relished our freedom for sexual
exploits and affairs. It is the giggles which always come alive
when I think of you.

It's painful to remember that tense awful day when we went to
the cancer specialist. Even then you managed to get the giggles as
you swallowed the dye and it was no wonder the nurse misheard
your age by 20 years. Instead of openly showing your devastation
at the final terrible diagnosis you winked at me and whispered,
'All those lovely young Doctors, Sue. I hope they don't drug me
when they're prodding and probing.'

That's why when you phoned later and started talking about

your will I thought you were still joking. I didn't realize its seriousness until you told me, no ORDERED, that I never reveal to anyone, in any circumstances, about leaving your secret fortune with me. We'd often chuckled about your athletic exploits with your hideaway fella in the Isle of Man – I called you the Minx of Manx – but it never occurred to me that you were hiding money away there too. Or perhaps you weren't. Maybe he did give you tips when you dressed up for him as a waitress and a naughty schoolgirl. My mind has been working overtime thinking what you had to do to earn £10,000!

I felt stunned when we'd finished speaking and I sat quietly trying to visualize the amount, having a job to keep it from Roger... Even though I'd had my orders I don't think I would have told him. Dear old Roger, sweetie though he was, he was still a banker at heart. In five seconds flat he would have invested it, trebled it, bonded and secured it. He liked you, though I shall always be grateful to you for pointing out that no one ever marries the nice guy.

Above all the money represented security. I didn't immediately think of a big spending spree, but saw possibilities of having a break for freedom, away from Roger. It was such a fantastic amount of money in my mind as it had taken three very difficult years for me to save £1,000. It was very mean of you to deny me the pleasure of thanking you personally but I don't suppose either of us realized that would be our last lucid and private phone call.

I know this is written three years after your death and the money never materialized. You had no way of knowing that your private treatment was going to cost you your public and private fortunes as well as your life. At least you were able to die in dignity at home instead of becoming the morphine addict you nearly were at the District Hospital, and I was able to sit with you again in the lovely soft bed. When you first mentioned the money you told me laughingly not to wish you dead yet. How those words stuck in my throat as I watched your grey painridden face with its faded laughter lines.

It's now dawn and I feel peace at long last – with myself and the world and most important, with you. It has taken this long to adjust to not having you here, our silly phone calls and our madcap holidays seeking those elusive millionaire playboys. I like to think of you chuckling over my shoulder reading this but most of all realizing that I still love you dearly, with or without your fortune.

Your niece and great buddy,
Sue

(Mrs J. Grant)

Dear Daddy,

This weekend Terry and I are going to a fellow New Zealander's wedding and I must write whilst I feel as I do.

She was telling me that her sister is here with her husband and that they will be at the wedding but because of the distance, and money I guess, neither parent is able to make the journey. Her brother-in-law is to give her away as the only male side of her family that can stand in for her father here.

Her day will be one of such mixed emotions and I think I know exactly what she is experiencing.

I know what you are thinking. What, apart from the obvious connection, does all this have to do with you?

Dad, she is so upset that her father will not be there to give her away and when she was telling me I was suddenly back to my own wedding day eleven years ago and those thoughts and feelings I felt hit me in emotional waves as if it were yesterday. All the things I'd wanted to say – special things a girl says to her dad on her wedding day – that I had unconsciously saved, and you were also not there to hear them. I promised you then that I would write to you specially and I never did.

I bet you don't remember the day you and Mummy decided I was old enough to go to the Shop all on my Own. It could only have been 400 yards. To me it seemed like four miles. I started out so full of my own importance; proud that I was considered such a Big Girl. I think I got two thirds of the way and then the enormity of it all hit me. I flew home sobbing. Both of you must have been frightened with the noise I made.

I can remember it as if it were just the other day. The postman bringing in the parcel for Miss Toni Boyce and giving it to me personally. You had gone back to work after helping to calm me down and had stopped at the shop, bought a packet of jelly beans, wrapped them and given them to the postman who delivered them within the hour. I couldn't wait for the other girls to come home from school so I could triumph over them.

My first day at school was similarly fraught. I was so excited and scared; you took me in the Austin and let me stand on the running board all the way. Even I knew what Mummy would have said if she had known.

One of my favourite stories about you is the one when you

bought the Surfcaster and we tried it out in the creek. You caught the most enormous eel and then – ugh – you landed it as if it were a fish. Remember who caught it fair in the face? Daughter number four standing alongside, screaming her support. 'Never mind,' you said as you wiped the slime off my livid red cheek, 'that will count as a full hiding – next time you deserve it.' I saved it for about six months. I can still see their faces as I was allowed to sit it out as my sisters 'got it'. We all seemed to get into trouble together didn't we?

Then, when I was nineteen, I had The Big Break Up with Paul. You came into the bedroom and gave me the keys to Your Car. 'Just drive to wherever you want. Blow all hurt away,' you said. That unforgetable drive did ease my heartache and I came back calmer. I loved you very much that night, Pops. Mum was furious she'd never been allowed to drive your car.

When I bought my own car the next year you lent me the money and charged me interest (to teach me the value of money)...That compound interest sure compounds. But I was grateful, I would never have saved so furiously on my own initiative. Going to England was so much easier because when the time came the money from the car virtually paid my fare. All I had to do was get the spending money together.

Dad, you were a great Father – the best a girl could ever have had. I was always proud of you. When my friend goes down the aisle on Saturday you will be in my thoughts.

Incidentally, whilst it's all on my mind, do you remember saying to all of us girls that you'd give us $500 if we climbed down the ladder and eloped? Well I was wondering if getting married in a sort of foreign country and doing all the food myself counts. $500 times 11 years at interest compounding – plus three children, wear and tear – I make that approximately very expensive.

Much love to you and Mum.

> Your loving fourth,
> Toni

> (Toni Gillan)

Dear James,

I was not pleased when you told me you planned to sell 'four dirty postcards for a pound' through an ad in *Private Eye*. It is not the sort of career a mother envisages for her son. However, when your brothers explained to me that you buy plain white postcards and dip them in a bucket of dirty water, I was mollified.

What career did I envisage for you when I changed your nappies, dressed you in your first school uniform, nagged you about 'O' levels? In my wildest dreams you were a lawyer, a pilot, an accountant. That shows the limitations of my middle-class imagination. As I bathed your cut knees, washed your rugby kit, shut the door on the tip that was your bedroom, I never foresaw that your first pay-cheque would be from the DHSS and you signing on every fortnight.

But you are tall and beautiful with your long hair and beard, and you look stately in your Oxfam suit. Your friends are weird and mostly incomprehensible to me, as I must be to them. I don't know how you fill your jobless hours, but you do.

Your brother Paul just came in after midnight. He and Charlie were out celebrating. Just as they were trying on a litter bin that looked like a space helmet a policeman came along. 'Is that your bin?' Paul assumed his best Welsh accent and explained that Charlie was on leave from the navy, and he hadn't seen his best friend for six months. Fortunately that was an understanding cop. Paul's poly course starts in a fortnight. Four years of business studies – it's a race between finals and his surviving brain cells.

Mike and the twins are back at school. Mike is full of good intentions, like confining his hangovers to weekends. Rob is glad to be busy again, after the long holiday. Philip, the youngest of you by twenty minutes, is the only one who has his career planned, and with his goldfish, canaries and the dog we have half a zoo already.

We all went to see Mike in his play. Rob noticed a very pretty girl in the cast (blond, interesting face, neat figure) and said, 'Mum, I'm in love!' It gave him the necessary incentive to buy some new clothes, so the next day we bought an outfit for him in the sales – canvas trousers, olive sweatshirt, white shirt and trainers, yellow socks. He looks lovely! but the girl has gone back to Scotland.

Having five sons is more fun and less hassle than you would think. I've been looking after you for 85 years now, but fortunately your lives are concurrent. It has sometimes been hard to make the money go round, but love never needs to be rationed – it's the only thing that multiplies when it is shared out. When I look at you all, tall and handsome, fit and friendly, I can hardly believe my luck.

Sometimes I am in danger of taking your good health for granted. When you had your appendix out I was frantic to see you ill. You weren't allowed to drink for three days after the operation. You were so thirsty you drank your mouthwash. 'Kill or cure,' you said.

Do you remember when you broke your arm at the age of six? We only noticed because you winced every time you hit Paul, who was two years younger. You enjoyed the X-ray and the plaster. You had to hit him left-handed after that.

The nicest compliment I've ever had was when a friend said, 'You give me hope; you're living proof that there is life after maternity.' It delights me to discover that too. I love my job. Every morning I get up and off to work with enthusiasm. I tell the boys, 'Find a job you like doing and get someone to pay you for it.' Writing the charity's newsletter and raising funds to help homeless children is an enjoyable challenge. But sometimes I get tired, working full time and having a houseful to feed every evening. By the time I cycle home from work I've run out of steam. When you were all in school and I was at university I must have been the only student who cooked for seven every night.

For recreation I've been constructing my own private heaven. In heaven there will be room service, and good food. I'll take my turn at the cooking but someone else will always wash up. There will of course be something to drink. All my friends will be in heaven and nobody will be jealous. There will either be no aggravating characters or I shall have developed an indifference to them. There'll be a lot of laughter and friendship; plenty of work to do (I don't want to be idle) but I'll have ample energy and only feel tired at bedtime.

There will be books and music and trees, mountains, grassy slopes (and I will be young enough to roll down them) and rivers.

There will be the scent of bonfires and roses and no petrol fumes. We'll be able to fly. There will be all the different nationalities and territories (without conflict) because I shall want to travel, especially if I have wings.

Speaking of travel, I'm entering a competition in *Cosmopolitan* to win a £5,000 holiday for two. I plan to set out for India on the Orient Express. I'll send you a postcard (a clean one).

Hasta la vista!
Mother

(Eileen Dight)

Dear Grandma,

My mother is a right old fusspot! Do you know she must have changed my nappy at least twenty times today? There I am playing happily on the floor emptying Mummy's handbag when whoosh, I am suddenly airborne, legs dangling, socks half off and transported upstairs. She whips my panties down, such an indignity, removes my lovely warm, wet nappy, pokes me about with cotton wool and greasy, slimey stuff, then whoosh airborne again. Well it takes some getting used to, all this fussing!

Anyway, how are you Grandma and how are Grandpa's specs? I didn't really mean to sit on them when we came to stay, though I did enjoy my holidays with you. Can we please come again soon? Maybe next time we shall be able to go to the beach so I can play in the sand with my bucket and spade. It was horrible that it rained so much this summer but I did enjoy digging in Grandpa's flowerbeds instead. Are his dahlias feeling better?

Mummy took me to the clinic last Friday and guess what? No! I didn't 'wee' in the scales this time, but I was pronounced a real fatty. I now weigh 21lbs 6ozs. How's that? I hope you are pleased. You should see some of the goo Mummy concocts for me; for instance, last week she mushed up liver (ugh) with cabbage (double ugh) and then became very cross with me when I spat it out down the back of my high chair. Well I do not think you would eat it either. I much preferred the meals you made for me, especially the fresh salmon with mayonnaise. I am a baby of taste.

Yesterday we went to see the doctor. I thought I was for the cold stethoscope treatment at first, but I was spared this time, thank heavens, it was Mummy's turn. Don't worry Grandma, I don't think there is much the matter with Mummy. I did have a lovely time in the surgery though. The doctor gave me some lollypop sticks to play with, but she must have given some other children the ice lollies to eat which I thought was a bit of a swiz.

Daddy is fine. Now that I weigh 21lbs 6ozs, he is not so good at tossing me in the air which is a real shame. He has been doing some repairs in the kitchen this week which has been great fun. He has been using his lovely tool box which is full of lots of interesting things like screwdrivers, measures and spanners. I think tool boxes are better than handbags.

Grandma, can you knit me something a bit more trendy please?

I'm getting a bit big now for those little white, lacy coats. Can you knit me something in loads of different colours and if you must make me a hat to match, please don't make one with a huge bobble. I get so embarrassed when we go to the clinic.

Can we come and stay for Christmas please? Your house has a chimney and ours hasn't. It would be so much easier for Father Christmas to visit.

LOTS OF LOVE TO GRANDPA. (I thought I better write in large letters in case his specs have not yet been repaired.)

Thank you for a lovely holiday Grandma.

Lots of love,
Baby Laura xxxx

PS Mummy sends her love.

(Mrs Dorothy Ann Twitchett)

Dear Ma,

Have just given up on the emancipation of the Russian peasants in 1861 and started into the late-night film, the ironing, a cup of coffee and a packet of Ryvita. Wet, windy Sundays and the *Economic History of Europe* (Cambridge Edition, Vol 6, Part 11) do not make for lighthearted living. Sal is completing the final paragraph of the eighth copy of an essay due last term. She is going to be one of those authors who write one slim volume, perfect and above criticism, translated into 55 different languages and read by three-year-olds, the world over.

On Thursday we 'Saved the City'. Two anarchist friends of Sal's arrived up from Liverpool, all flower-power dungarees and a lack of soap going back to the days when Mummy stopped glowering over them in the bathroom. We joined them at a meeting on Tuesday and partook in an anarchist plot to disrupt Manchester's economic system. If all anarchists are like Sam and Pru they really need all the support they can get. She is afraid of the dark and had to acquire a boyfriend on her first night at the poly because she can't sleep alone. At two o'clock in the morning they crept into Sal's bed, abandoning our three star front-room floor, because Pru was sure she could 'feel a ghost'. The resulting chaos has led to a reappraisal of Sal's ideas on anarchy, communes and even family life.

Pru and Sam live with a trainee Buddhist monk (converted from the Presbyterian, no less), his revolutionary Communist party mother and her young Italian lover. The Buddhist monk has to traipse off every morning to his monastery and clean out the communal bath, light candles under it to heat the water and then, when everyone else has had a scrub, he can have a wash. Any notions I've had of becoming a Buddhist monk have disappeared for good.

Pru and Sam, as well as rushing around redirecting hares or foxes who might get in the way of passing hunters, are fruiterions – that is they only eat things that fall from the trees, mostly bird shit in Manchester. They explained to me patiently that you could gently lift things from the tree rather than stand underneath with your mouth open. Apples, oranges and nuts are acceptable so long as they are untouched by South African hands. It certainly simplifies the diet.

The anarchist meeting produced at least 12 likely-looking revolutionaries; their mission, to stop all business activities in Manchester on Wednesday, changed to Thursday because of prior commitments. Outside MacDonalds was the venue, 9 o'clock the psychological moment. Unfortunately due to lectures, we could not join the revolution until after lunch.

When we arrived Market Street was teeming with revolutionaries. Punks with orange hair, Animal Rights workers dressed entirely in plastic and already steaming gently, political aspirants, a women's group and several CND badge wearers, all handing out balloons, stickers and free advice. Several pavement artists had already staked their claim to prime sites. We arrived just in time to take over the Stock Exchange. The porn shop had already had its doors superglued and Barclays Bank was having trouble with the cash dispenser. We dropped stink bombs in the street, smoke bombs in Lewis's and piled all the trollies in Marks and Sparks with meat and decorated them with Animal Rights leaflets. We got a brief rest during the anti-nuclear demo, when all that was required was that we lay down in the street looking dead until the end of the three-minute-warning period. Then we jumped up and ran around singing to passing shoppers.

Perhaps it was my singing that tipped the balance, but the fuzz arrived at this point and arrested the smallest bloke they could find accusing him of violence. We all trooped off to the police station and waited outside to see what was happening to Jimmy, while the guard duty copper insulted us – 'If any of you had half a brain, you'd be dangerous.' Clearly the average policeman needs a creative thinking and language enrichment course. We sang to him too – he called in reinforcements. Singing is more dangerous than I had previously thought. Why didn't you warn me about it? Now I know you'll take their point of view, but it does seem ironic that the moment you start to think or say anything about what we do to animals at the ICI plant or to comment on the stupidity of two countries amassing enough weapons to annihilate the world when two-thirds of it is already dying of starvation, they call you brainless and irresponsible. Still, all in all, a worthwhile day.

I felt protested out and have since started an undercover literary career as a reviewer for the college mag. We saw an all-black cast play to an all-black audience (except for Sal and me trying to look as darkly freckled as possible). I wrote a deeply felt and meaningful piece about the show and had it accepted without reservations. Came home elated to find that I had been completely wrong in my interpretation according to Sarah, who is an intimate friend of the author, the director and the entire cast and may set the incitement to misunderstanding committee on to me if she reads what I've written. Another career closes its doors to your ever dutiful daughter.

Please enclose spare five-pound notes, new knickers and fresh sirloin steak in your next letter from home. Send more stamps if you wish me to continue with these reassuring epistles.

Yrs exhaustedly,
Jane

PS Isn't education broadening my horizons!

(Janet Whitehead)

Dear Dad,

I stayed with Auntie Mary last weekend and, looking through her old photographs, I found some of yourself, as a student and enlisted in the navy during the war. You looked very handsome then – a kind of Rudolph Valentino good looks, which must have had the women swooning. Did they? But, of course, such a suggestion would embarrass you. You never did like personal references.

I've gathered that you were a very shy young man, a farmer's boy lost in the city, with dreams of a quietly distinguished career in a university somewhere. I can see why Mummy fell for you.

It must have only been a few years later that you were a headmaster of a small village school, with three children and a wife to keep, and your dreams creeping away like shadows in the sun.

I look at those photographs, and see my eyes in a different face, and fearing that I might also have inherited your tendency to blow with every wind, I turn to another page in the album – your wedding day – and watch Mummy's face, as though she was still alive. She was strong, wasn't she? Oh yes – and wilful, and independent. Fancy you of all people marrying into that strange matriarchal Cornish clan!

I don't have any quarrel with that young man in the photograph, or the old man you are today. I quarrel with the man who sold his daughters for the sake of a quiet life – sold them to a woman who stripped them of their teenage years, who indulged in every sort of petty, middle-class cruelty, a woman who punished them for being Jessie Trevorgan's children. And when we were locked in our rooms for some imagined misdemeanour, sent to school in the bits and bobs from jumble sales, told we were only 'lodgers' in the house, made to clean and look after her children all our waking hours – where were you? WHERE WERE YOU?

I saw a silly film on late-night TV the other night and the father said to his son, 'I'm proud of you' – just general Hollywood 'goo' – but because I'd been thinking of those photographs, I thought, 'I would have liked my father to have said that to me.' You see, I am 40 now and it must be at least 15 years since I last saw you, and, although I have your eyes, I have Jessie's firm jaw and *I* am a strong woman, too. I have two beautiful – and wilful! – teenage daughters. We live together with my man-friend of ten years in relative harmony, in a terraced house which looks out over the Atlantic Ocean. We all went camping last week and, despite the rain and mud, the girls dressed in glorious clean pale pink trousers and twitched their bums up and down the promenade, with the local boys never far away!

I used to teach like you – now I run my own youth club and when I walk in the streets, people know me and greet me.

And about all this, you know nothing. I intended you to know nothing. You lost your chance to be proud of me years ago.

You see, I don't really believe in forgiveness, New Testament style. I could visit you tomorrow, you and your wife – and we would have a polite tea and make polite conversation. We wouldn't talk about anything that really mattered. And when I went away you could be satisfied that you really had made contact with your daughter and therefore the past would be negated. NO.

I like the Old Testament with its burning bushes and its grand and fearful notions of revenge.

This is my revenge. Although I will sometimes look at the old photographs and see my eyes in your face, I doubt if I will ever send this letter and I will definitely not be coming for tea.

Jess

(Penny Windsor)

My Dearest Son,

I feel I must write this letter in an attempt to explain why I made the decision, from the very beginning, to conceal the desperate seriousness of your illness from you.

As your mother, I felt I knew you better than anyone; that if hope of a cure was taken from you you would be unable to cope with what lay ahead of you. Since you no longer had a future, I could see no virtue in destroying your present.

You never seemed anxious to discuss your illness, although a boy of your intelligence must have realized how bad the prognosis was, and you chose not to divulge your innermost feelings to anyone – perhaps this was the only way you could cope with it.

How glorious was the summer of '84. The sun shone increasingly and Fortune seemed to smile on you. Your love of horse-racing, which you took *so seriously*, paid rich dividends which you swiftly exchanged for super golf clubs; a new guitar; fine recording equipment; rare Dylan tapes – you had the Midas touch and I rejoiced with you and for you.

On that fateful Friday when my world turned to darkness, we were all enjoying a splendid vegetarian lunch (you were a food freak!) and your appetite was enormous . . . the voice on the phone said: 'The results of Tuesday's biopsy are very bad. Lawrence has a highly malignant tumour and we are as yet unable to locate the primary.' I felt faint with shock – you asked me who was phoning and I lied swiftly (how adept I became in this skill in the months that followed), 'Oh, nurse has been delayed. Dr M will do it himself at 5.30 p.m. . . . more salad?'

Later that night, alone in your room, you sought comfort in Dylan's music and decided to try the orthodox treatment recommended for you.

The treatment was harsh and you changed from an energetic, athletic young man into a round-shouldered, shuffling wraith with a deathly pallor, but the doctors all talked of a cure . . . I alone was not convinced.

Christmas was fantastic, since I was certain it would be your last and you, although so frail, played your part magnificently. On New Year's Eve you were half crazed with pain which you later confessed had been gnawing at your back, 'like toothache', for weeks, but you were determined that everyone would enjoy this Christmas whatever it cost you.

The bone-scan result was very bad, the cancer had spread to your spine, ribs, breast-bone – no one mentioned cure any more, palliative treatment to control pain was now the sole objective. We had some bad times getting the pain sorted out – you reacted to the radiotherapy badly and your weight kept dropping. You were, by now, so exhausted that we took you for treatment and then straight home to bed.

In a desperate, last-ditch effort, some suggested chemotherapy, you jumped at the chance. It was so harsh that you nearly died at Easter so, after a harrowing skirmish with a senior consultant who wanted to tell you you were doomed, I decided to take you home and nurse you myself. I knew how much you hated hospitals.

You were confined to bed by now, savaged both by the cancer and the treatments so I brought you into our lovely bedroom and surrounded you with all your treasures. Kept open-house for all your young friends who rallied to your aid magnificently.

Miraculously you improved, regained your appetite and some weight – lurched through to the sitting-room, painfully, on a zimmer – such progress! We indulged in daydreams, about what you would most like to do when you were better – you used to say: 'When I've licked the *Big C* let's make for the *Big A*, then Nashville and New Orleans. We might even get to see Bob Dylan in concert.' How your eyes lit up at this for Dylan's music was, without doubt, a source of comfort and strength to you to the end.

Thanks to a homeopathic doctor, you were no longer sick and the pain was well-controlled – we were even talking of a remission. My birthday came in July; you gave me a super Polaroid – 'idiot proof' – managed a piece of cake; even the sun shone . . .

But a month later, *animala dimidium meae,** you were dead. I was with you, loving you; cradling you in my arms; I came as far along that lonely road as any mortal is permitted to. Should I have told you immediately that you were doomed? Prepared you for death and deprived you of all hope? This is the modern approach and I had a hard time fighting their determined efforts to ignore my wishes. Had you had a wife and family, financial commitments, the decision would not have been mine. But all you had left was hope and it gave you five more months of life, within limitations, that no doctor thought you would have.

In maintaining this façade, I paid a high price: denying myself the relief of showing my grief to anyone, playing the fool for your sake, unable to tell you how proud I was of your quiet courage: struggling to eat when nauseated, to walk when every movement was agony so that you could spend your evenings with the family. You maintained your independence and dignity right to the end.

Only in your last hours could I tell you how much I loved you, my darling son; the plans and dreams I had for you; how good a son you had been to me; how dark and empty my life would be without you. I asked you to forgive me for keeping the truth from you, my dearest. You see it was my last gift to you – a return to those golden days of childhood when Mummy was the omniscient centre of your universe and able to protect you from all harm.

If I caused you pain or sorrow by my determination to nurture hope in you right to the end, please forgive me, for it was the final expression of my overwhelming love for you.

Till we meet again.
Your ever loving Mum
*the other half of my being (Horace *Odes* III)

(Mrs Carmen Demarco)

Dear Mark,

You have now been at boarding-school for a fortnight, and we take it as a good sign that you're too busy to write! Your telephone calls have given us snatched glimpses of your new life – its excitement (you're in the football team), its new opportunities (you've learned to play bridge), and accounts of strange experiences – I quote, 'The French master is totally mad. He speaks entirely *in French*!' We hope to learn more when we see you next week, but meanwhile your old-fashioned mother thought you might like something more lasting than a phone call, more private than a tape.

You've already discovered that books can yield repeated pleasure, and that the best can be read again and again. So it is with letters. And if an author can communicate with his readers who are total strangers, how much more contact should there be in a letter from a mother to her son? But perhaps that close relationship can leave important things unsaid, for fear of embarrassment or breaking taboos.

So if by writing this I'm changing the way we look at each other, think of it as a step forward, an inevitable development. Life is about growth and change – after all, you look very different now from the crumpled red person I first met in hospital twelve years ago! You've never previously spent more than a week away from us, so it's a fresh experience for us all. But I think you were ready for more responsibility and will rise to the challenge of this new adventure.

I'm sure you will cope because you have already displayed great self-sufficiency and common-sense. Your training in the Cubs and Scouts has been a help here and you have relished making your own decisions. Choosing a course of action and then committing yourself to it is something than many adults find difficult, so I'm proud that you have the courage of your own convictions.

Another factor which will stand you in good stead is your ability to make friends. You appreciate people's individual characteristics and enjoy their differences. In a world where many are insecure and can find companionship only with cloned versions of themselves, your zest for life is truly valuable.

You also possess a sense of humour and an imaginative

approach to life. The former makes you cheerful and optimistic and a fun person to be with. The latter is crucial in a world where stereotyped responses cause many problems. If you can look at people and situations and offer a new perspective, this means you can make a worthwhile contribution to the welfare of all.

A quality which I like to think you inherited from me is your enjoyment of self-expression. We both love poetry, art and drama. The worlds of fantasy and illusion are as enticing to you as they are to me. The magic of the theatre is a pleasure we both share. I hope you have the chance to do plenty of writing, painting and acting, as achievement in these areas is immensely satisfying.

You can see we have a good deal of confidence in you, and we hope that your education will develop other qualities we have only glimpsed so far. One of these is patience or stamina, the ability to stick at a task until it's finished. You show this when you paint a miniature, but you need to take the same attitude to work you find difficult – e.g. Maths or French! We know you are always keen to improve a story, and will rewrite episodes until you're satisfied – but this might not be the case with something you find less absorbing. Your new environment will be helpful in offering you good working conditions.

We chose a Quaker school for you because we felt its caring philosophy will matter more and more as you grow up. Already you have your opinions on world affairs and each generation must try to put right the mistakes of the past. Working for peace and serving one's fellow man are noble aims which we hope you will adopt as your own.

If this seems a rather solemn letter, remember that we are looking forward to hearing your jokes again and seeing what has happened to your hairstyle. The dog misses you and tries to sneak upstairs to sleep on your bed. However, the rabbits have had a peaceful time without your football battering their hutch.

As you can imagine, I am thrilled to bits that Matron is doing all your washing and sewing. I hope she has also checked that your toothbrush is used for your teeth and not to paint your Dungeons and Dragons figures. I dare not enquire whether showers are compulsory.

Have you eaten my fruit cake yet? As you know, I don't usually make cakes, but it seemed the right sort of thing for your tuck-box. If it's rock-hard, bring it back and I'll give it to the Junior School Autumn Fair.

Your brother is making a video tape of all the TV programmes he thinks you would like. So although you should be acquiring a good cultural background, you can ruin it all by watching hours of rubbish when you come home!

We look foward to seeing you and hearing all your news.

Love from Mum

Dear Mom & Dad,

You will be surprised to receive this – our phone calls seem to be more instantly reassuring than letters, and laziness has a lot to do with it, but somehow, lately, I've felt a real need to clarify my feelings both for myself and to you.

The last few conversations we've had have had what I think of as a 'glass wall' effect. We were talking, but not communicating, and this left me with a sense of flat frustration which until now I have had difficulty in understanding.

Did I imagine it or was there a feeling of defensiveness and restraint about your replies when I asked you how the current situation was affecting all of you.

Please, please, understand me – I am not attacking you or accusing you (you see how insecure I am!!) but feel bewildered and hurt. It is as though after six long years of feeling cut off from you by so many miles, desperately isolated at times of festivity and of crisis, I now feel an emotional gulf opening between us because I somehow think that you see me as either judgemental and condemning, or smug and self-satisfied, finally vindicated in my decision to leave.

I love you both so much and I want you to know and understand that the agony and uncertainty that you and all South Africans, both black and white, feel is mine too. Yes, I have been exposed to a different way of thinking and my studies have shown me a different interpretation of the historical and socio-economic context of what is happening. This does not mean that my trailing roots will ever really recover from being torn up, and the ache for all that I have left behind will ever subside. The brown, barefoot, carefree days of my childhood will always be with me, catching my breath with longing sometimes, as I realize that they are lost, never to be relived through my own children. I can only recreate them with word images – the peppery smell of highveld dust and the summer-dry crackle of yellow grass underfoot. As I write I hear the sleepy call of turtle doves in the Cape, and see the blue gum trees etched against the hot blue sky as we clambered on the slopes of the Heldenberg – searching for old Voortrekker wagon tracks scored deep in the solid rock. You must remember the time the mountain mist came down as we walked on the narrow path, wrapping us with chilling suddenness until we stumbled out of it, our panic melting in the sunlight. Childhood memories must always be poignant, but somehow they feel intensely so, knowing that those I shared them with are back there in that remembered landscape and that I have made the decision to spend my life elsewhere, bringing up my children far from the warmth and continuity of grandparents and family close at hand. Their roots are here now and so will their children's be...

Please *never* imagine it is easy or comfortable for me here at the moment, my interest and concern is never detached or objective. I will never be able to remove myself emotionally from my homeland, no matter what intellectual experiences and national arguments I am involved in.

Please let me share this time with you, don't let me become an alien to my family as well as to my culture. Caring is all we can offer each other and my deepest concern is that, whatever happens, the experiences and love we share between us will let us reach each other at this time.

Your loving daughter,
Diana

(Diana M. Bass)

74

To future generations who never knew me,

Perhaps you've seen some faded pictures of me and someone has said: 'That's your great-grandmother' – well, there was more to me than a faded picture! That's why I've decided to write this letter introducing myself, because a lot of what you are stems from me, and I wonder how many of my characteristics you have inherited?

I wasn't always old, grey or dead! At the time of writing I'm thirty-one and the year is 1985. Don't worry, this isn't going to be a history lesson. If you want to know about Britain in the 1980s visit the library. This is your personal introduction to me, as a living, thinking human being, not some dusty relic from the past.

I have two children, Simon who's nine and seven-year-old Joanna, and we live in a lovely chalet-style house in a little Scottish village called Neilston, so forget any visions you may have of your ancestors huddled together over a bowl of gruel in a remote Scottish croft because life is very pleasant. Simon and Joanna attend the village school where they are trained on computers and I work as a reporter for the local newspaper. I love my job passionately and I'm a great believer in freedom of the press which means I can indulge my nosey nature to the hilt in finding out why, who, where, how, and when, and get paid for it! I'm also a great writer in everything from shopping lists, letters and books, to my diaries, which I hope have been passed down and will have already provided you with hours of amusement.

I divorced Simon and Joanna's father after six years of marriage simply because we made each other miserable. He was in the Royal Navy and I was in the WRNS when we met, and motherhood followed quickly afterwards so we married for convenience. Yes – we did have contraception in my day ranging from pills and coils, to sheaths and various other methods, but Simon and Joanna arrived regardless. Anyway, the marriage trapped and stiffled me and I don't believe in paying for one mistake for ever, but the divorce did leave its scar which could have been avoided with a little more foresight.

After the divorce, I returned to Scotland from England and lived with the children in a tiny council flat less than a mile from where I was brought up. We had little money (save your tears! this was the norm and we didn't starve) and we lived on social security which was money from the state. I use the term 'lived' loosely. We survived on social security, but as an eternal optimist I saw this period as a temporary 'setback' and not as the end result.

I managed to find a part-time job in a discount supermarket and wrote endless articles to newspapers and magazines to help make ends meet, but for a long time life consisted of work and sleep with little money for luxuries. Just when things were hitting an all-time low both financially and emotionally I met Hassan. He may or may not be your great-grandfather for at the time of writing we are not yet married, but let me tell you – he was wonderful! He was an Iranian scientist and we met purely by chance. By the second date I knew no man had ever shown me such warmth and kindness and we fell very much in love. But we made an odd combination and suffered a great deal of pressure from his family. It was clear I was not good enough for him. He was an eligible bachelor with a Ph.D. and immaculate background and I was a working-class single parent living on social security with a council flat and two children. On my side, gossips considered the fact that he was not 'white' juicy enough to make life miserable, especially for the children.

Three years later, we bought the house we are living in now and are blissfully happy. I have a good job and a certain amount of status, but tags like 'golddigger' and 'single parent' are hard to live down and cause a great deal of hurt.

The children stay with my parents at weekends which gives us some precious time to ourselves. Sometimes we hold a small dinner party and serve Persian food, or visit the theatre or a quiet country pub, but mostly we just relax and make love.

So you see, the faded pictures tell you nothing of the person behind the smile. Long before you were even thought of, I was laying the path for your future. Whose grandchildren are you? Simon's? Joanna's? – or perhaps another child of mine who at this moment lies in the limbo of my future.

People don't change much and a hundred years from now it will still be the same. I once read, 'Life is too short to take seriously, and too short not to.' Don't take your problems too seriously and if you live your life to suit yourself don't do it at the expense of others.

Remember me as a stunning redhead with green eyes and a

sharp wit who loved life, money and success, and tasted them all however briefly. I was once like you and I had a ball! Don't waste a precious moment.

All my love from the eternal optimist, your great-grandmother,
Yvonne

(Yvonne Burks)

My Dear Nephew,

When can I stop calling you that? How long has this affair been going on? Well, I will tell you, six years this December! Six years when I have bitten my tongue, actually, I would have bitten something else given half a chance!

This letter, my dear, will help to make me feel better and of course enlighten you.

Shall I tell you about the times when I have cooked you a meal, knowing you had to go home and eat another one? Or the times when realizing your weakness for the bottle I have given you much more than I have given myself, so that you would be unable to drive home. There was also a time when, invited to your house (she was working), I sprayed your bed with my perfume on the way back from the bathroom. I have also sprayed your clothes with the same perfume. Feeling faint yet my dear?

Remember the car crash? I was driving, you of course should not have been in the car; the lengths to which you were prepared to go to hide that fact! You even asked my friend and neighbour if you could pose as her husband when the police came!! I ask you! I then put your name down on my insurance form and, my God, you hit the roof, telling me I should have put a false name and address down. My dear fellow, someone must be worth protecting!

Yes, whilst we are about it your excuses to the 'lady at home' read like an entry in a joke book. The one you told her about staying in the car in *your* garage all night, remember, that was the night I set the alarm for 5 a.m. I had to wake *you* up to go home, You arrived home washed, dressed, unrumpled. Wow, you must be a fantastic liar, come to think of it, you have had rather a lot of practice!

Remember the conversations we have had – the one that started 'I wish you would/could find a man to love you', tell me dear, how!

The last time I tried that, you kept turning up unexpectedly. You even went to the pub with him one night and between you decided that you would continue to see me. Just as well I love *you*!

Oh, remember the classic one? 'She' was working for a cosmetic firm in a local store, you kindly suggested that it might be a good idea of I go in and have a make-up done by her! Below the belt a little, don't you think.

The phone calls, we must remember those. She must be more than a little deaf. How many times have you phoned me late at night – to wish me 'goodnight'? I have usually been sleeping – you are mostly very drunk and she, my dear, asleep upstairs, you hope!

When I lived at home, the phone calls where you put on a false voice and gave a false name; idiot, you fooled no one, least of all my poor parents. The times when we have been out and seen people we know, 'I have just bumped into Viv – haven't seen her for ages.' Who the hell are you kidding!

How about the time when you wanted me to hide under the table in the restaurant because you saw someone who knew you 'both'? You were quite upset when I refused.

How many postcards, Christmas cards, birthday cards have you got from 'Aunty'? Quite a few, dear heart! What about the two sets of friends you have? I am sick of making excuses for you, at weddings, parties, etc. I end up going alone, have to put my own name on cards, presents, etc, in case someone recognizes your name.

People must think I lead a strange life. I am sure most of my family think I am gay, or a dedicated career woman. Where are you when I am asked such questions? Happily living out your other life!! How can I begin to tell them, 'you see there is this man but...'!

Yours sincerely, X

My Love,

Odd not to know your name. We could pass on the street without a glimmer of recognition. Yet you're part of me – more than anyone else in the world.

Today is a special day, your 18th birthday. Our relationship is older than that. None of the intervening pain has managed to mar the memory of its beginning. The magic of it has survived intact. I'd like to be able to send it to you, wrapped and ribboned, marked FRAGILE.

It was a lovely day, my favourite sort, crisp and golden. Your father and I drove into the country, happy to be together. Ireland is beautiful. Have you ever been there? I wonder . . . But it was a stolen day. We'd both lied to grab it. Being in love made lies easy to justify.

His wife didn't understand him. I was your age and had yet to learn the commonness of that ailment.

Things change. The mellowness became a memory as wind and rain stripped the trees of their finery, leaving them stark and bleak. I'd never seriously contemplated pregnancy. Oh, I knew all the facts, seventeen years of farm life had seen to that. But I was in control. 'I'll help you get rid of it.' That's all I can recall him saying. Blame is easy to fling. Love can turn so swiftly to bitterness, but bitterness destroys. He wasn't a bad man, only afraid, and weak, just as I was.

I couldn't tell my parents. Their disappointment and forgiveness would have been harder to handle than anger. And so I found myself on the ferry, off to a new job, as far as they were concerned. Your father was true to his word. I was equipped with a fat wad of money and an address he'd got hold of. Our paths have never crossed since.

That journey – I've never again been able to face it at night. Where were all the people going? The noisy drunks petrified me and the weary, white-faced women, burdened with bags and crying kids, seemed to reflect my own despair. The smells and the motion had me fighting nausea before we'd left the harbour. Downstairs it was hot and stuffy, up on deck it was bitterly cold. Leaning over the rail the mesmerizing oily swell seemed to offer the obvious solution. No one would know. But the thought of my parents, waiting and waiting for news of their daughter, immobilized me.

The night passed. I must have been a pathetic spectacle, trying to look as if I knew where I was going in Euston Station. A woman approached me and started to talk about God. I mustered up enough strength to be rude, but her eyes stayed kind. I took her little booklet and fled.

The room I found became my womb. It was dingy, but cheap, with four walls, a bed and a door that locked. Here began, in earnest, the battle for your right to exist. That battle raged for five long, cold, lonely days. I tramped miles of London streets, searching for an answer to a question that wouldn't go away.

I had to be practical. One mistake...erase it...start again ... learn my lesson...start again. It would be better, better for you, for me, for everyone. No one would know...start again...yes, better...Abortions weren't as commonplace then as now. They certainly weren't as publicized, but neither were unmarried mothers.

Finally I made my way to the address. I was ready to do the sensible thing. Did you know? You protested. It was the first time I'd felt you moving. Instead of going to the doctor I found a café and sat a long while over a mug of tea and a sticky bun. Ridiculous – it had the air of celebration!

By then it was too late to go anywhere but back to my room. The walls closed in and the panic returned. That woman in the station, she'd known, her eyes had shown it. The booklet – 'Read it,' she'd said. 'It's part of God's word.' God? Who, where, what was God? I found it, still stuffed in my duffle bag, crumpled. Psalm 139 – that's where I opened it. Time hung suspended in the words.

> For you created my inmost being,
> You knit me together in my mother's womb...
> Your eyes saw my unformed body...

Could they be true? A life, your life, in me, could I dare take it? Then the tears came. In their wake came sleep, that benevolent obscurer. Probably for the first time we rested together in peace.

The decision was made. Now all that remained was to live with it. I got my job and kept writing home. Those letters –

masterpieces! It helped to let my imagination take flight and paint for my folks the sort of picture they'd like. I was glad they never asked me for a photo. And I knitted. I didn't want to let you go, as I knew I must, with nothing of your own. And I wanted whoever got you to know how loved you were. All the while I was conscious of those unseen hands silently knitting form into you. We grew together.

Today is a beautiful day, ablaze with sunshine and flowers. A good day for a birthday.

My love,
X

(Hazel Archer)

Dear Richard,

I think I can finally, at long last, say that – 'Dear Richard'. I wouldn't have been able to a year ago, for instance. If I'd sat down to write this letter then it would have begun with a howl of pain and anger – more along the lines of HOW DARE YOU! How *could* you? How could you leave me like that – without a word, a warning, a clue? I felt so abandoned, so deserted. Betrayed.

But I think I've got rid of the anguish now. I think that's gone. I still *miss* you of course, and wish you here, but it's a gentler, more accepting feeling. I can now look at people who knew you with (almost) detachment. Without that feverish longing to suck and drain them of their memories of you. I used to will them to mention you, but stumble if they did.

It's fifteen years now. And six weeks. It was such a glorious hot August day, the morning they buried you. (You see, I still think of it as 'they' – I wanted no part in it – I resisted it with every fibre of my being.) When they brought the coffin to the house (it looked so *new* – it was such a surprise that it should be brand new, specially made), I wanted to hug it and to hit it and to rip it open and drag you out. (Did you know that the dog howled all the time we were at the church?)

I wore that scarf that you brought me back from Paris, do you remember? and I lost it that afternoon. There was a violent storm – very dramatic, the sky went black and the heavens opened. If I'd read it in Thomas Hardy, I'd have been sceptical. At the station there was a huge poster that said 'Richard's Had An Unfortunate Year'. I think it was for an insurance company.

At least you visited me in dreams. Though that was a mixed blessing: sometimes it was agony to wake up and realize that it was only a dream. And you know how selfish I am – I had nightmares that They would get *me* now and squash me in a wooden box and nail it down.

One dream I had twice: I was hanging around with a group of friends – there was a sense of waiting for something. Suddenly you walked in, looking sheepish and apologetic. You came over to me and without a word being spoken you said you were sorry and I forgave you; then we all held hands and formed a circle and were complete, whole. Odd that it happened twice, as though you had to tell me twice. You always were brainier than me. (I?)

You were better than me at everything – except art. You were a better *person* – more tolerant, more compassionate, more caring. Did you realize just *how* ignorant I was? You did *try* to educate me, I know, but I wasn't very receptive, was I? I left 'all that' to you, like the wife who leaves the voting to her husband. Dreadful. I tried to make up for it later...

In fact, I sometimes wonder if you bequeathed me some parts of you in some mysterious way. I don't mean my maths has improved or I've taken up the cello – but I did go off travelling and become much more independent, my own person. Mind you, I think the travel bug was a form of running away and came from very selfish motives – talk about intimations of mortality! I was consumed with a greed to see everything and do everything.

Did I always want you to go on ahead, or does that impression only come from knowing you were born first? Once or twice I've been tempted to try that re-birthing lark – can you imagine?

ME: Go on – nip out and come back and tell me what it's like.

YOU: OK. I'll fetch you if it looks reasonable.

And you never came back, so they had to fish me out.

We had a good childhood, though, don't you think? I have a scene in my head of the two of us being pushed around the garden in a wheelbarrow – but I may just have seen a photograph. I do remember rolling and tumbling in a mountain of fresh grass cuttings when we'd just moved to the farm, so we must have been four. All those marvellous stories we dreamed – in our world, down the field, along the stream and into the wood. Do you remember the wigwams we built, year after year, amongst the bracken, before the bluebell patch? What about that time we were late and Ma lit an old firework and it came soaring out above our heads?

The terrific things about twins is that you're never really alone – there's another one of you, out there somewhere. I didn't appreciate it – you – fully, of course, until it was too late. A girl at school kept saying, 'What's it like, being a twin?' and I'd say, 'Dunno, really, 'cos I've nothing to compare' – serves me right for being so glib. There is something special about twins, though, isn't there? I still find our birthday difficult and I never know what to say when people ask about brothers and sisters. Am I still a twin?

It was bloody good being one, though, kiddo. You were very patient with me. I was very proud of you. Do you remember going into that pub and the rugby team calling out, 'Hey, different one from last night, Dick!' They wouldn't believe we were brother and sister, let alone twins. You were so much taller than me always and you were looking so *good* just before you died – broad shouldered and all that hair. Wish I'd got a photo. And then you went on ahead, again, and still you haven't come back for me.

Love,
Jen

(Jen Coldwell)

Dear Rhoda,

   This is a very difficult letter for me to write, which is why I
have waited for so many months to write it. In fact I only feel able
to do so now because I know your American name, as well as the
Israeli one which David gave us for their engagement
announcement.

   I have wanted to write to you from the moment Elizabeth told
us she and David wanted to get married. I knew that this
marriage would upset you, because you do not know my
Elizabeth. She is a lovely young woman: I would have said 'girl'
but, with the baby due so soon, she must now be given full status!
They are so happy together, she and David, and he loves her so
much; we knew this from when we learnt David had sent her
home to us when he was forced to leave her and continue his
military service and she was so ill in Israel.

   We knew then she had found herself a good man, and we
waited confidently to meet him and we were not disappointed. Of
course we were worried that he was Israeli and that he was
Jewish, but we knew that he was a good man because he had
nursed our daughter when she was so sick and infectious, and he
had sent her home to us when he could no longer look after her
himself.

   I tried to keep her at home with us, but the letters and cables
arrived so regularly and I knew she had a return ticket, paid for
by a man we didn't know, and I was afraid. Elizabeth is a special
child to me. Although, like you, I have four children, Elizabeth is
my third child and was born when my husband was away from
home; and, because I was lonely, I loved her more and had more
time to be with her. She was a beautiful baby – dark haired and
dark eyed and with the most gorgeous pale skin. She still has that
same beauty today and, although she is so big with the coming
baby, she has such a young-looking face for a twenty-year-old
woman. It is strange really – she has never been one for make-up
or dressing up, and she is still wearing her dungarees and
T-shirts, and from the back looks exactly the same as ever – but
what a shock when she turns around!

   Your Aunty Mary visited when she was over from Canada – it
was she who told Elizabeth your American name. She also told
her we hadn't brought our daughter up properly or she wouldn't

have gone to live with David as she did. This is not so: my husband and I are a very traditional couple; like you, we celebrated our 25th wedding anniversary last year and our lives have been devoted to our children. The children have strong beliefs: they value family life and look forward to marrying and bringing up their own children in a loving atmosphere. My daughter is not promiscuous: she is an intelligent, headstrong girl who, when she found the right mate, did what any healthy young woman might have done.

Of course we have been anxious and we knew there would be problems and, to be honest, I have wished a thousand times that I hadn't sent her to Israel for that 'year out' after her 'A' levels. We were asked for our blessing only a fortnight before their actual wedding day. And we begged them to wait three years for Elizabeth to complete her nurse's training. My husband said to me afterwards how tired Elizabeth looked that weekend, and it was then I guessed she was pregnant. They were so worried in case when David's visa expired they would be separated, and so anxious to secure their future together that we relented and helped them to get everything together as quickly as possible so that they could be married.

What a week that was! My husband and I hardly slept, and how I envied my friend whose daughter was to be married in the village church to a young accountant from the next town. David was desperate to be married in a synagogue, although Elizabeth was happy to be married in any church. My husband is a Methodist and Elizabeth was christened in his church, though I am a confirmed member of the Church of England, and Elizabeth has always attended a Church of England school. None of us had ever contemplated a registry office wedding, but Don and I knew from the start that this would be the only sensible way for Elizabeth and David. We were married in my parish church: me in white, and both families joining together. That is the way it has been ever since.

My husband's family rallied round for Elizabeth and David's wedding, as did mine, and it was almost a perfect day. The only sadness was that David came to us on his own. We know that he has a loving family and that his father is a traditional, religious man; but I guess that you must understand what Elizabeth has done. She, like you, left her own country when she was a young, impressionable girl and fell in love with a handsome Israeli soldier. That was what shocked me most, actually, that she loved him when he was a soldier: all my children are pacifists and Elizabeth has been very active in the movement for many years. However, love knows no boundaries, and fall in love with him she did and I hope they will remain for the rest of their lives as much in love as they obviously are now.

We are all sad when we think of the shock all this must have been to you. I felt grief that my daughter wanted to marry a man from a totally different culture from our own. I felt deprived of the traditional church wedding I had anticipated for her, and now of the joy of seeing my grandchild wearing my grandmother's christening robes and receiving its name at the font. But, having worked through this petty grief (for that is now what it seems to me) I thank God for the lovely son we have received into our family.

David visited us last year – a long-haired young man staying at our home on his travels through Europe; he returned in October and stayed until New Year. We knew then he would marry Elizabeth: they were so right for each other and such good friends. I begged him not to move to London: he had no money, no job and no friends there. But he wanted to make his own way in life and he went. When things got tough he rang to tell Elizabeth he was leaving the country, and she just said: 'I'm coming to you.' And she went. They returned together a few months later to ask Don's permission to marry.

This weekend David's old flat-mate, Hyam, is over from Israel and they have brought him to visit us. What a different David! He now owns business suits; his hair is cut short and he drives a car, which I understand is half-owned by the company for which David works. Life is not easy for David. The baby is due in a matter of weeks; Elizabeth is tired and David has held his job as a salesman for only a month and the strain is showing on him. He is trying so hard to do the right thing by his wife and the coming baby, but now more than ever he needs to know he has your love and the support that a united family can give.

I suppose you know Elizabeth has been taking instruction since she was in Israel, and learning Hebrew too? Last week she visited a rabbi in London to discuss the process of conversion. She is very anxious for David to be returned to his family and knows that there is more chance of this if she converts to your faith. We, as a family, are very keen to meet with you and your family. We realize there will be difficulties with regard to food and habits; we are willing to observe all the necessary courtesies; and, indeed, we have found since knowing David that our interest in and knowledge of his culture have broadened our minds considerably; there are lots of questions we wish to ask you with regards to this.

None of my family has strong feelings about Elizabeth's wish to convert; but, knowing her as I do, I feel she will come to resent being accepted only if she converts. She is a person of strong feelings; her love for David is very apparent, perhaps when you see them together your grief will abate and you will realize that if David loves her you can too, even if she isn't 'one of your own'.

Perhaps I may never send this letter; but if you do receive it I want you to know it is straight from the heart of a mother, not only of daughters but also of a son. I cannot always approve my Antony's actions (he is, by the way, David's age) but I always will love him and I know that the love of one's mother is a very strong support and an encouragement in the face of adversity.

Anne

Dear Alison,

I hesitate to write this letter, as I know it will upset you, and yet I must let you know how we, your father and I, feel.

We love you, and we only want your happiness, remember that.

I felt numb when you told us last week that you were leaving Brian for another man. I couldn't believe it, I thought that you were so happy together, and you have only been married for 18 months.

How could you leave Brian for a married fellow, the father of two young children, and he's on the dole.

You say you have no feelings left for Brian, Alison. It seems such a waste, please try again, you may find a deeper, loving relationship.

Brian has told me he wants you back, he loves you, and would still want you if you'd had a hundred lovers. True, enduring love like this is hard to find in these days when divorce is so easy.

You have always been your father's favourite (he was really stunned when you told us). One of his happiest moments was when he held you in his arms, only a few hours old. He was 24 then, and I only 18, six years younger than you are now. We had to get married, things were different then, in those days it was a disgrace. But we loved each other, and weathered the storms together. We worked hard at our marriage to give you and your sister a happy home; it was our pleasure to see you and Sue secure and happy.

It was my crowning moment to see you walk down the aisle on your father's arm, he was so proud that day. When I thought back to my own hurried registry office affair I was so happy things were different for you and you had a better start. We helped you set up a lovely home together, and were always there if you needed us, but I was careful not to phone or call too frequently, I didn't intend to be an interfering mother-in-law, as we loved Brian like our own son. Alison, please think of your lover's wife and children; if he has any love for them you may feel always second-best, if he has no love for them he is worth less than nothing.

It may be the last thing on your mind at the moment, but think of the financial aspect, you will have to think of it sometime. You may have to help support his wife and children, and when will you be able to afford children of your own? Can he support a second family? It will be hard for you, I hate to think of you having to struggle, you have always had the best we could give you. Please give your marriage a chance, 18 months is not long enough; don't do anything rash that you may regret later, just stand back and think what you are throwing away.

I hope you may have second thoughts if you consider the situation fully. Alison, please remember love comes not only through an hour's passion, but through years of sharing and putting the other person first.

It may be unfashionable to think this way, but I sign myself,
Your old-fashioned, but loving Mother.

Darling, we will love and support you whatever you decide, you are still our daughter.

To my dear unborn child,

Today has been a very special day in my life, because I saw you for the first time when they did an ultrasound scan on me in hospital. You are only 14 weeks into your development as a human being, following our conception of you in June. What makes the whole experience all the more incredible and special is that only months prior to falling pregnant with you, we were told that it was unlikely that I could bear a child as I appeared to be infertile. Can you imagine the joy when I was told by the doctor that the pregnancy test was positive – you, my little miracle, had been given life!

I also had the thrill of hearing your heartbeat today. It was most reassuring, like the constant ticking of a clock as the hands of time turn round. I also saw your profile on the scan – the shape of your tiny head from the tip of your chin, up over your button-sized nose to the top of your head, and down the curve of your back with your body extending into long, shapely legs and arms. You weren't still, as I had imagined you would be, but madly swinging your arms and kicking your legs as if you were swimming in the amniotic fluid you are bathing in inside me.

It occurred to me that you seem to have vigour and a fight in you to survive – you must have, with all you and I have been through these past weeks. As you know, I've suffered from chronic sickness and have lost a stone in weight since you nestled inside me. Yet despite the pummeling you've been taking from this unfortunate side-effect of the pregnancy, you've been growing steadily and I'm assured by the doctors that you appear to be in good health. This discomfort is worth it just knowing that in 5½ months' time, God willing, you will be delivered into the world.

We are already preparing for your arrival. I've started knitting for you and have already received gifts from kind friends and relatives on your behalf. You are going to have some very attractive outfits to wear and are assured of sleeping snugly, as we've already received three beautiful hand-crochetted blankets for you. Other than plans for your bedroom and your wardrobe we have no preconceived ideas for your future existence. We only want you to be born healthy and fit. For the rest of your life I hope your father and I will be good, loving parents to you and all we want for you is that you will be happy. After all, I believe the mark of a successful life is really just being happy.

It is my intention to keep this letter somewhere safe and to give it to you when you are older – perhaps when one day you learn that you have given life to a child – either carrying it yourself if you are to be a girl, or through your wife if you develop to be a boy. I have no preconceived ideas of which sex you will be and, in fact, have no preference either way. Sometimes late at night I lie awake and wonder what you will look like – whether you will have my fair hair and blue eyes, or your father's dark hair and lovely olive green eyes. Perhaps you will take after your grandparents and have brown eyes! It's very exciting waiting to see how nature has fashioned you – I know to us you will be beautiful.

I wanted to write this letter to you, although you will not receive it for many years, but when you do finally read it I hope it will express to you the love and joy that your life has represented to me. When you do finally arrive, you will really have been the greatest gift I've ever received in my life.

Till then, all love from your
Mother-To-Be

(Mrs Rosemary Koumi)

Dear Auntie Agnes,

How do I reach you, a prisoner of your own nature? A letter? A telephone conversation? I ring, I write, but I cannot truly touch you.

Spinster daughter, casualty of an age in which the youngest took responsibility for an ageing parent and there was no future for the 'unattached'; possessor of an Elementary Education, which equipped you for only the most menial of tasks. Always predisposed to be a natural victim, never able to take up life and bend it to your will.

So, you took a lifetime learning how to vanish, how to fade away before the random blows of Fate. Now, you scream alone in solitude and silence. You fear the doorbell and feign not to hear the telephone ring.

Your erasure of yourself is nearly perfect, you have become so elusive as to slip through every net I create to catch you out. You hate your home but are too afraid to leave it. You describe your plight in words but will not let me help.

Your letters are your only real salvation, a vehicle to carry all your cares. At this distance I am removed enough to bear your confidence; I cannot intervene and am thus considered 'safe'.

I care for you but dare not ever voice it. I shall not come, I must not intervene. I know your mute appeal is for me to remain faceless, to be a 'someone' who will read but not condemn.

So, please go on, dear Auntie Agnes, to use me. I will remain remote, a mere audience to your own interior monologue; a narrative which I hope will never end.

> With love,
> Mary X

Dear Laura,

For a four-year-old you understand a great deal about life but what is happening now is beyond your comprehension for the time being. This letter is for you to read when you are old enough to understand about love and feelings and will hopefully reassure you that the reason daddy and I are no longer living together is by no means any fault of yours.

When you were born in September 1981 you were a living symbol of the deep love we felt for each other and our joy and togetherness at that time were communicated to everyone associated with us. Friends commented on the almost tangible glow that surrounded the three of us as we proudly shared our triumph with them.

This happiness was to be ours for the first three years of your life as we watched you grow and develop as a person in your own right.

Sadly, slowly as life seemed to quicken pace and daddy and I began to be caught up in the tangle of career, mortgage and constant financial pressures we began to isolate ourselves from each other. We remained parents but no longer partners and finally, this summer, we painfully admitted to each other that we were no longer in love. Our goals were no longer the same; our paths no longer meandered peacefully along together.

We both suffered great anguish as we tried to protect you from the bitterness we felt; we knew that you intuitively recognized the barren wasteland that was our relationship. You had tantrums, you sobbed silently for no apparent reason and you clung to us for support.

At four years old you mourned the loss of our love as we selfishly fought for our own individual self-respect and bickered over legalities.

But we never for one minute stopped loving you Laura, and we guiltily regretted the effect our disintegrating relationship was having on your childhood. On many occasions you discovered one of us crying and silently you hugged us or slipped your tiny hand into ours. At such times our love for you would overcome all selfish fears and uncertainties and make us determined to protect you from further pain.

I know that when you are older and more aware of the

technicalities of divorce you will wonder why your parents separated, leaving you with a mess of a family and denying you the chance to enjoy large family occasions because one parent will always be absent. You will become tired of explaining the details of your dislocated family.

How will you cope when we each choose to share our lives with a new partner? Will you always resent the newcomer's claim on each of our affections? Will we constantly have to make excuses to each of you about the other's behaviour?

Will I ever forgive myself for including you in such a frightening situation? Can you survive the trauma and walk the fragile tightrope to emotional security?

Laura, you are a beautiful, strong, determined little character and I trust you will understand from this letter that neither daddy nor I ever meant to distress you. Hopefully we will both grow from this experience and be strong enough to communicate our deep commitment to you. We live in a terrifyingly insecure world and I want you to feel safe.

Our love for each other may have paled but our love for you will forever be a bond that will unite us. We will delight in your triumphs, console you in times of doubt and be there when you need us.

There will be times when you wish daddy and I lived together again and I am sorry that this cannot be. But rest assured darling that your home is with each of us and that however far apart we may be our thoughts are with you.

Be Happy,
Mummy

(Beverley Anne McLeod-Turner)

Dear man in a jam,

I was in a jam when we met, in two jams in fact, or three if you include my brother. The first being the one of traffic, the second (to my acute embarrassment) was the centre of the doughnut I was eating and the third, I've already said – my brother.

5.15 on Highbury Corner, it's the sort of place you'd expect to be stuck. On my left a 1950s Saab with an Ecology Party sticker, spewing excessive amounts of carbon monoxide into the earth's atmosphere and straight through my air vent. In front, the white American thing, two buses wide, in it a man who surpassed 'cool' and must have been freezing with the roof down and the gentle pitter patter of the English summer hitting his shades. Behind, a family of five, each hooked into their individual 'walkperson' – carried away from each other by the perfect sound of hiss free stereo.

That's where you came into the picture, well not so much the picture as the mirror in fact. Just in the edge as I tried to brush off the tell-tale grains of sugar from my face – yes I remember it perfectly, just a fraction of that godly face in my mirror, the merest hint of that jawline and those gleaming teeth.

Little brothers let one down on the most important occasions. What a moment to hand me another doughnut! and when I signal that I'd really rather not, he claims it for himself – taking the sort of 'big bite' that only a little mouth could take – and successfully squirting strawberry jam over my face as he leans in to 'see what I'm starin' at in the mirror'. How do *you* respond in a crisis? I distinctly remember doing rather well in that quiz – but that doesn't equip you to deal with being caught in a jam with jam running down your face, your little brother in the seat next to you and the most beautiful jawline you've ever seen in the rear view mirror.

So I clean up my face with as much dignity as the strawberry jam allows (God bless mother for leaving the Kleenex in the car, I had accused her of being 'pebbly' at the time), and I make a determined show of authority by grabbing the doughnut from little brother and hurling it out of the window. Glancing in the mirror to check that my face had returned to its normal sickly pale colour as opposed to the puce pink of combined embarrassment and strawberry jam I was consoled.

Imagine my horror on seeing the unmistakable sight of red jam dribbling down that most sensuous jaw. A direct hit.

So I turn to see you. Up there. On a bill board. Fully two dimensional. Ruined by a well-aimed doughnut. I laugh. Oh hilarity. The tears of little brother drowned by the tears of my laughter... Beep beep... the angry noise of those behind who can only see the disappearing car in front and not the joke. Beep beep... as I stall hilariously... Beep beep... as I get the car to shudder forward... A big long beep as I turn around to see who in this world it is that is too busy for a joke in a jam – and then, without warning, you winked.

See you at Highbury.

BT
the woman from the jam

(B. Obsfield)

THANK YOU

Dear Dr Whitehead,

I am writing to thank you, you are a remarkable woman Dr Whitehead. It is all because of you, with your rosy cheeks and old school tie, because of you and your jolly disposition reminiscent of many a bully-off on the school playing fields, that I was able to undergo my very first cervical smear test. At 27 years old I had never managed to go through with one of these dreaded examinations.

I am not generally cowardly. I once let young Dr Richards down at the surgery examine my backache, so it wasn't really cowardice that prevented me from rushing off to a 'Well-Woman Clinic' – it was more like complete terror. I have been in the grip of this for 9 years. It was the thought of having a pair of sugar-tongs wielded at me from the wrong end and then a thing which they say looks more suitable for viewing Halley's Comet – in fact for a moment there Dr Whitehead I thought you were going to erect a tripod and we were going to pass a very pleasant hour or so chatting about the sky at night.

My first smear test at 27; you may gasp at the prospect that I had managed to slip through the medical net for 9 years, taking the pill willy-nilly and assuring myself that I'd get examined next year and then next year and so it went on. My mother, who treats these examinations as she treats buying a loaf, roars off down to the surgery every 6 months to harangue the frosty-faced receptionist for smear-test appointments and I think this must have provided some sort of smokescreen for me to hide behind.

Then came the scare. Headlines screamed that the smear test was very vital and no woman should be lazy or irresponsible enough to ignore this simple safeguard. My friends – the inner circle – threw up their hands and virtually signed a petition to implore me to make The Appointment. Their descriptions of the event were numerous, ranging from 'there is nothing to worry about – you'll feel so good afterwards, better than passing your driving test ...' to 'they only strap your ankles to posts when it is really necessary ...' Posts? What Posts? Anyway, I tried to be selective in who I listened to and then picked up the phone and dialled your number.

I am still amazed that my legs managed to carry me through the portals of your surgery that morning. If old frosty-face hadn't checked me in so sharply – it was touch and go there for a moment. My legs were heading towards the door, my brain was cajoling me to sit down and wipe the sweat from my fevered brow. I had contemplated a hip-flask but the thought of guzzling down neat vodka at 9.30 a.m. in the waiting room, in front of mothers and toddlers, was too much and I was also afraid of being incoherent, unable to say 'cervical' and asking instead for a packet of nicotine chewing-gum, before staggering out, mission in ruins. No, I refused the offer of a valium, rejected the idea of asking if I could smoke throughout and steeled what there is of my willpower as I turned into the surgery. I had paraded up and down outside for 15 minutes, imagining that all the women drivers passing were thinking, 'poor girl, must be smear-test day ...'

And there you sat, dear Dr Whitehead, your hair in a slide and your cardi buttoned up wrongly. I can vaguely remember muttering in dry-lipped panic, 'I've come to have a sm ... and some nicotine chewing-gum please ... no, I mean a smear test.' From then on it was plain sailing, as they say – no posts for my ankles, no sugar tongs, no device from Jodrell Bank. It was all as the dear friends had said, over in a flash, completely painless and the humiliation factor was cut to a minimum, all thanks to your nice line in chat and truly professional approach. My friends are all very divided over whether the doctor should be male or female; most girls/women seem to feel strongly about the sex of their doctor and stressed their preference strongly, arguing with anyone who disagreed. Only one dear friend, who is just this side of being completely batty said she didn't care if ET did it, as long as the results were okay.

So, Dr Whitehead, you were picked as you can see after much deliberation and although I may have appeared calm and nonchalant, in my very long T-shirt (recommended because 'you're not left standing there with it all exposed while they put their gloves on') it was in fact, for me, quite an ordeal and had been planned, discussed and analysed down to the last detail.

I do not think that I thanked you sufficiently at the time; if I could have given you flowers I would have. It was like getting what you want at the hairdressers and tipping everyone in sight gigantically. In the newsagents on the way home, in reply to the lady assistant's 'what's up dear, fagged out?' I told her of my achievement. She patted my hand and said 'Oo it is an ordeal, I know, but we're so lucky to be able to have it.' These words were a revelation, not so much the 'fagged out' bit but the 'lucky' – a word never before associated with 'smear test' in my mind. Resentment maybe, that if men had to have it there would probably be a scanning machine invented which would let them keep their Levis on. 'Lucky' that was a new angle and, in the light of it all, I think yes, it is a very appropriate word – I only wish that others like me and I know that they are out there, shivering in their timbers and laden with guilt and anxiety, would step forward and not be afraid to take The Smear Test Phobia by the horns and wrestle it to the ground – it could save their lives. I also hope and pray, that there are a few more like you, Dr Whitehead, out there to greet them.

Yours sincerely,
Carolyn Trevivian

Dear Doctors,

Now that I'm back in the security of a daily routine, I want to look over the past months and tell you exactly what I liked and disliked about your treatment of me in and out of hospital.

You knew I'd already had a benign lump removed from my right breast at another hospital the year before, but this time something on the mammogram made you suspicious. (By the way, does a mammograph machine have to be as comfortable as a giant thumbscrew?) Not that I believed it would be any different from last time – until the male nurse who filled in my admission form and took down all my intimate details started talking about how good 'falsies' were these days! (At least the surgeon didn't patronize me at your hospital. When I had the first lump removed, I had wanted to make sure that, if it were malignant, I wouldn't wake up breastless; the surgeon sneered and told me I had been reading too many women's magazines. Also, that time, the staff nurse asked me who was my next of kin just after I'd had the pre-med. Nice timing!)

No, you were much more human about the whole ordeal. The ward was relaxed and friendly. We even had a small choice of menu. It must be very difficult for you, though, to tell someone they have cancer, even though they're reasonably young and the tumour is below critical size. It was a shock to me and I could see you wanted to move on as quickly as possible, leaving the nurses to comfort me. They did; those young girls put their arms around me when I needed to cry and listened to me when I needed to talk. Next day you didn't even acknowledge my existence when you came to see another patient. You are a good surgeon, though: thanks for the small scar.

But this is where the story really starts ... I must congratulate the specialists on always taking time to sit down and talk over any aspect of the post-op treatment or any worry I might have had about the illness. I never thought so much time would be given to a National Health patient. Also, I congratualte you on the thoroughness of the tests you gave me to make sure no other part of my body was rebelling or to check up on some of the weird ailments I developed.

I ought not to complain; it's just that there are a few niggles left in the back of my mind.

First, why did no one warn me that the gentian violet dye used to mark me for radiotherapy would come off all over my clothes? (A gold star to my boyfriend: he called these marks my 'road map' and said that they were your way of passing on where the next doctors' party was to be held. He was never put off by the marks or scars.)

Second, why were mild chemo-therapy and hormone therapy presented as if they would have more or less the same side-effects when chemo is much more unpleasant to undergo? (I know the answer to this one: you were conducting a research survey and didn't want more women to choose one treatment over another. In fact, women couldn't choose – they were allocated their treatment randomly.)

Third, why did no one explain, until after I had started chemo-therapy, that it might (just might) bring on a premature menopause. I'm only 33 years old; I would have liked to have been informed.

This is all past me now. My body wouldn't take the chemo-therapy – the blood count stayed too low. So now I'm on the much easier routine of one hormone tablet twice a day and fewer hospital visits.

But I know you'll be there if I need you and I know you'll act quickly if more cells get out of hand.

And, of all the doctors at all the hospitals, I'm glad I got you. May your government grants never run out.

With kind regards,
yours sincerely,
Janet Braby

Dear Doctor,

It was twenty years ago, almost to the day, that our relationship began. For the past two decades, through sick and thin, you have cared for me. Ours has been the most stable relationship in my life – forget the husband, parents and child, they are too unpredictable. You, on the other hand, with your gentle touch, your quiet voice and sympathetic ear, have been the perfect foil for my rebellious and delinquent body.

I'll never forget our first meeting. Nine o'clock on a Monday morning. I staggered into your surgery, one side of my face lower than the other, one arm almost useless, and a definite list to the right when I tried to walk. No, I wasn't drunk, I'd had a stroke! You were so calm: 'I think we'll let the hospital have a look at you.'

Well, it took us nearly a year to weather that storm, but during that time we laid the foundation stone of a wonderful medical affair. Then came the marriage break-up and my break-down. Needless to say, you were there with your guidance, understanding, and tranquillizers. Heavens, I must have been in a state. You only prescribe those as a last resort! This period of turbulence in my life lasted much longer and I still feel the tremors from it.

We progressed through bronchitis, cystitis, colitis and many other types of 'itis', our relationship growing stronger by the ailment. Then followed a quieter period in our lives. We saw less of each other. But this was a false calm, soon to be shattered by the hair falling out syndrome.

'My God, doctor, I'm going bald!'

A reassuring, 'How many bald women do you know?' put our relationship back on a more even keel, but my terrible torso had another card to play. My hair turned white, practically overnight. It grew in from the roots, and a broad white stripe appeared down the centre of my head. On this visit to your surgery I looked more like a demented skunk than your usual long-suffering patient.

'I can't go white at thirty-three, doctor.'

'I'm afraid there's nothing I can do for you this time.' Then, as an afterthought, 'but I'm sure it will suit you.'

For a while after this we took each other for granted. Life ticked steadily forward. I remarried; you continued along your healing way. Then, one day back in the haven of your office, 'I'm pregnant, doctor.'

'When's your period due?'

'It's not – for another two weeks – but I know I'm pregnant.'

Four weeks later, pregnancy confirmed, you and I faced the most serious decision of our time together. To have or not to have the baby. Since the stroke episode I had been taking Worfarin to thin my blood and to undertake pregnancy was extremely hazardous.

'I'm going ahead, doctor.'

'You always were a gambler. I'll do everything I can to help.'

We took the pregnancy a week at a time. I grew more confident as the months went by, but you for once were not prepared to say 'you should be all right now'.

Once again, however, with you beside me, I made it against all the odds. How I appreciated your unexpected visit on the day of my son's homecoming. If possible, you were almost as delighted with him as I was. 'You've done really well there.'

'Thank you, doctor – very much.'

I suppose that's really what this letter is all about. It's one great big thank you. We still see each other over the occasional bout of coughing or sneezing. You and I are just entering our menopausal phase and I dare say we'll survive this too.

No, I haven't fallen in love you with you, doctor – not quite, but I am most grateful for the special role you have played in my life. I could not have come through without you.

I now look forward to the next stage in our lifelong 'affair'. I wonder what challenging surprises my body will throw up in our mature years. Nothing you can't handle I'm sure.

It seems strange to say I look forward to seeing you next time I'm ill. Nevertheless, it's true, because visiting you is like returning to a tried and trusted friend.

> Yours in sickness (and in health),
> Sue Roper

PS I think I have an ingrowing toenail. I must make an appointment!

Dear Doorman at Wimbledon Town Hall,

I am writing to thank you for your excellent show of gallantry when I passed out, outside the Town Hall. Despite mumblings from onlookers about me being a drunk or a drug addict, you came to my rescue most heroically. If I had been in a better state of health I could have stood up for myself, and explained to those most helpful people, who were so concerned about missing the 93 bus, that I was, in fact, merely suffering from side effects of a typhoid injection administered to me that morning, and probably from the eighty-degree sun which was blasting down like a hot furnace at the time.

I am particularly grateful to you for being a good Samaritan as I am sure you will agree that as a swooned young woman, scantily dressed in summer attire and carrying over a hundred pounds in cash after an aborted attempt at a shopping spree in Knightsbridge, I was particularly vulnerable.

You took me under your wing into the cool stone-floored reception and sat me down with a glass of water. There was not a hint of a blush in your cheeks even when a pair of giggling females clopped passed and up the stairs, whispering something about 'the old guy doing all right for himself'. You didn't ask me personal questions as to how I came to get into this state of nausea, but continued tenderly to hand me sips of cool water until with genuine delight you announced that at last some colour was flooding back to my cheeks.

For days after I contemplated walking in and plonking a bottle of Scotch on your desk, or sending you a letter, and even sending you a postcard from my honeymoon destination of St Lucia, for which the dreaded vaccine was intended; but alas I let all these go.

So dear sweet man, here at last is my long awaited THANK YOU.

To you I am eternally grateful.

Yours sincerely,
Marianne

(Marianne Louise Blackshaw)

Dear Wayne (or is it Shane ... or is it Garry?),

Wayne will do. You won't remember me but you changed my life this morning. You were so golden, so gleaming with your white teeth and curly hair. Mills and Boon would be happy to have you in their stable of heroes. Bet you even have a cheek muscle which tightens with passion.

There you were, bare to the waist, shovel in hand, hacking away on an approach road to the M25. There was I, boringly clothed to the waist, driving wheel in hand, coming back from the doctor's. The headache was worse, splitting as they say. Was it a tumour, early stroke, multiple sclerosis or just terminal exhaustion brought on by two toddlers, a job and an ambitious husband.

The letter I was planning to write was the one to the children; something of me that they could read when they were old enough. I would tell them that despite my tragic early demise I had already had a lifetime of pleasure from them. Which of my friends would make a good stepmother? Someone plain but kind, a homemaker, doing all the things I never did – cakes and gingerbread men, ironing sheets and cleaning ovens. No glamorous, high flyers for my children, though Nick might have something to say about that.

So you see Jason, sorry, Wayne, things were pretty bad as I put my foot on the brake to negotiate the corner you were standing on. I looked up, you looked down, eyes met and you *smiled!!* The headpains vanished, ten years dropped off my age and I had a future again. Many thanks. The M25 is bringing us many blessings in Essex: quick access to Heathrow, 25% increase in house values and glorious young men who smile at women in cars. Hope it's never finished.

Love,
Christine

(Christine Baxter)

Dear Sirs,

I am writing to thank you. First of all for the marvellous work that you do for unwanted and unloved animals. Secondly, for Tappett.

He started life as an unwanted puppy, kicked out on the streets of London. We came to Battersea one day, looking for a two-year-old bitch. Tappett came home with us in a cardboard box, eight weeks old, male, brown, soft, and absolutely gorgeous.

He was always playful and loving. He used to open the fridge and raid it whenever there was a chicken carcass inside. His puppy teeth were found on the landing, embedded in a lump of Stilton, but the backs of all my smart shoes must have tasted better.

He didn't like me having a bath, used to sit on the mat and bark until I got out. When he grew out of that, he slept across the threshold in case I needed lifesaving. One day guard duty must have been too boring. He sneaked into the bedroom, and chewed a hole in my diaphragm, and then hid under the bed with the evidence.

When we moved from the flat to a house, he loved the garden. The only trouble was, he turned it into something resembling a bombsite by digging holes, nay craters, everywhere. When he'd finished that, he would hop over the fence and take down the next door neighbour's washing. Unfortunately, this must have been about the time the rot set it. Reports were received that he'd taken twenty sheep for a swimming lesson in a pond. Luckily no damage was done, but he did come home rather muddy.

The day we brought the kittens home, he thought it was Christmas. They spat and hissed at him, but he hunted them out, rolled them over, and held them very gently with one paw for an all-over inspection. Tappett used to carry them in his mouth. The first time he took Tiny out into the garden, I thought he was going to dig a hole and bury him like a bone! But, above all, he really did look after them, and love them.

Scargill, the Mynah bird, had him a bit confused. He mimicked Tappett's barking perfectly, and whistled him every time a door was opened. No way would he stand for Tappett's nosey parkering either. Many a sharp peck on the nose was received in the course of valour.

When I moved away, I had to leave my best friend behind. It wouldn't have been fair to take him away from his garden, to a flat in the high street. But, after a few months, I came home to find him tied to my motorbike by the back door, wet and bedraggled, but oh so pleased to see me.

He immediately ingratiated himself with everyone else in the flat. Everybody, when they arrived home from work, got a kiss and a cuddle, and a big soppy dog on their lap. In fact anyone who came round got the same treatment. Unfortunately it proved impossible to keep him inside. He would jump out of a window, run across the roof, and down a fire escape.

The first time he did a 'runner' he was reputed to have been sitting on the zebra crossing in the middle of the high street, stopping the traffic. He always crossed the road on the crossing. Big day of the week was Friday. Friday is market day, and he always went out to lunch, numerous portions of scrounged pies and sandwiches.

He became a regular in the pubs in the town. Often getting there all on his own, or before us. Apparently he went on a pub crawl with the Royal Artillery, when they were in town for the Carnival. When the Carnival was on, we even boarded up his window to keep him in, but he still turned up in the meadow.

He never missed out on anything that was happening. We went to the Donkey Derby, Tappett was there first. My brother had to borrow a piece of string to tie to his collar from the dog display team, otherwise he would have joined in.

Everybody in town knew him. I would go shopping, and people that I didn't know would be saying hello to Tappett and giving him a pat. His biggest claim to fame was that he was the only dog to be rescued from the roof of the local supermarket by the fire brigade. We never managed to find out how he got there in the first place!

Tappett was a smashing dog, a real character. He was loved by everyone who knew him, and he loved everyone that he met. Unfortunately, this letter is written in the past tense because he has been dead a month now.

Nobody could be held to blame. We had been to a barbecue on a sunny Sunday afternoon, and then to a pub for a drink. Tappett must have nipped out while I wasn't watching, and I didn't realize there were any sheep in the area. Somebody told me that he might be chasing them, so I went after him. As we got outside I heard the shots. I ran across the fields and found him. He was dead, my dog had been shot.

Tappett was 3½ years old, and was one of the best loved dogs ever. He may not have lived for long, but he had a wonderful life.

Thank you again.

Yours faithfully,
Sharon Lee

Dear Dr Luke – oh very much more than mere doctor –

Are you even there still? Do you, twenty-six years later, go on day by day performing your miracles, helping the barren to fruitfulness – or reversing sterility into fertility, as no doubt you would put it? Gowned, gloved and masked, you looked so alarming as I slipped away into anaesthesia for a half-hour that changed my whole existence.

Afterwards, you had gone; only nurses were there, benign in the relief of post-op, and I didn't see you again. I meant to write immediately the pregnancy began, to pour out the amazement – the incredulity after years of never-never, the gratitude for the one pair of hands that had untangled my problematic insides. But it seemed comic, ambiguous, impossible: 'Dear Sir, I have to thank for my recent conception...'

Even more, when the child was born, actually real, whole, perfect, I intended to rave to you about miraculous births and so on. That seemed too profane, though for me it would have been a cool understatement, so I put it off till a calmer moment. Euphoria is not to be trusted with the written word, especially in the uproar of a large maternity ward.

Rapturously home with the infant prodigy, the emphasis on cleverness began to shift, I regret to say, and life so completely changed that gathering together pen, paper and stamp was out of the question for the time being.

The orderly, jog-trotting mundane years of tea for two had gone for ever, everything was glorious, but chaotic and exhausting. Between feeds and sleepless nights I did manage to acknowledge the flood of matinée jackets, the woolly lambs, the rattles and bibs; but the much more important thanks, dear doctor, were never written.

Life moved rapidly on, and every analogy you can think of on the lines of 'great trees from little acorns grow', can now be applied to the family situation chez nous: the quiet backwaters of our settled married life, pre-baby, swelled into broad streams, rushy torrents, huge wide oceans. The rest of the world with its families, its experiences of childhood, schooldays, teenagery, studentship, all poured in and out of the house, the thoughts, the everyday existence of our next few years.

And all this richness because I came to your workshop for half

an hour and you defied the Fates, who presumably had decreed
otherwise for me, their origin being in the dark ages before X-rays
and advanced obstetric research. The wrath of the third of those
terrible sisters must have run extremely high when my son was
born; she, who supposedly cuts the thread of human life, met her
match in your superior skills. I know you will be unmoved by all
this attempt to set down at long last, my feelings on the matter,
and you will believe that you are just doing a job, like a bus-driver
or a civil servant or any other humdrum old wage-earner. You
will certainly not remember me, just one more number on your
list, though for sheer jelly-legged cowardice I must have ranked
high in your 'most difficult women I've ever had to deal with'
category.

How could you know, really KNOW, what it felt like to come,
empty-stomached, for the anaesthetic at 8 o'clock on a bleak
January morning, fearing it more than anything ever before and
hopeless of its outcome? To you, the whole theatre set-up was
utterly routine, your face, set grave as usual, gave out no
reassurance; nothing of the bedside charmer, 'we'll soon put you
right, have-you-pregnant-in-no-time', sort of banter. How I
wished for that, anything but the cold-blooded business of
climbing up on to that high table, all chromium and white
sheeting, petrifyingly aware that in two minutes time I would be
UNAWARE, temporarily dead, while unthinkably sharp
instruments would be prodded into me. No uplifting thoughts of
darling little babies, only sheer terror of the unconscious
moments.

You were, I remember, ignoring me like any butcher about to
go through the mechanical slicing up of a few chops; actually
making a little polite conversation with the Sister about her
forthcoming holiday – Portugal, a package, she chattered, whilst I
lay in acutest dread of the about-to-happen.

Could you have known how I loathed the whole hospital system
at that moment, but in particular yourself, with your remote eyes,
your detached air, your clever-dick ease with the surgical cutlery,
your mysterious authority.

And now I have found time, after the hurly-burly years, to
confess to such emotions so belatedly I cannot be sure you will
ever read of them. Letters writers are a threatened species, they
say, and this could excuse my too-long silence. This is the reason

my son always gives for not writing these days.

He did come home the other day though, for his quarter-century birthday, and we went together at his request to see the labour ward where he was born. People thought it odd. But as you know, he just might never have existed.

My thanks, and his.

E. Crawford (No.63710, 25 Jan 1959)

(Elizabeth Crawford)

Dear Father Mulvaney,

Thank you for changing my life! Extravagant as this statement may seem, it is wholly accurate – and one which you no doubt yearn to hear after Sunday sermons. The revelation for me happened some months ago, after watching you on Late Call: that religious panacea spooned out nightly on TV, heralding closedown.

After a particularly harrowing day at work I had stopped off on the way home for a large bottle of wine, 20 cigarettes and some peanuts, and spent the entire evening sprawled in front of the TV – fir, bathrobe and slippers on, cat on lap, other creature comforts within easy reach. I was mellow, almost sleepy by midnight when, to the strains of Handel's *Messiah,* your friendly-salesman smiling face appeared against a background of soft furnishings, soft lights, dried flowers and the cross. Having neither the energy nor the inclination to move, I stared, comatose, at the screen. I was at first bemused by your changing tone, the intensely sympathetic furled brow, the contradictory blood and thunder delivery. The monologue seemed to be directed personally at me as you spelled out your accusation in no uncertain terms. I was a sinner, a hopeless case. My one chance was to bow before our Saviour, admit my inadequacies, confess my sins, and repent. In exchange for my continuing self-deprecation, when the glorious day dawned and I would meet my maker, I would be thoroughly cleansed and saved.

By the time the national anthem struck up, I was reeling with a fusion of emotions. Infuriated, but with a calm sense of purpose, I walked slowly across the room, turned off the TV set, returned to my seat and drew heavily on my last cigarette (smoking it far closer to the filter that I would normally in these concious times). Wide awake now, I sat in foreign silence and began to sculpt the fragments of my fleeting thoughts into something as tangible as an opinion. Intuitively I responded loudly I DON'T BELIEVE IN GOD! Well, of course, I have known this for some years, but fired by your banal statements, I knew there was a logical conclusion to my arguments somewhere among the brain cells and the Rioja.

If there is no God, and therefore no salvation, what was my image of the afterlife? Blank. No, I was not stuck for an answer, that was my answer. Like God, I do not believe in the promise of an afterlife. No lost spirits weeping in dilapidated mansions, no doppelgangers, no light at the end of the tunnel nor reunion with long-forgotten relatives. My end would be marked by incineration (far preferable to becoming worm-fodder). How much more romantic for that grieving spouse to be able to wend his way to a fondly remembered spot, a cliff-top perhaps, and to watch his loved one whip away dramatically in a wild wind (not thinking of the poor chap on the other side of the ocean with grit in his eye). The End. No hauntings or visitations to ouija board fanatics. My spirit will remain the private property of those who care to recall my life, habits, quirks, idiosyncracies, my pros and cons. Suffice it to say, if I can't make my mark while I'm here, I sure can't make it after I've gone!

However, a prerequisite to any sensible debate you and I could have would be your admission to the fact that no one, not even El Pape, knows our fate after life. This is evidenced by the fact that you and your colleagues appear on late-night TV in an attempt to 'sell' God – just as other image makers promote their products. Of course the promise of an idyllic eternal life is a strong selling point but, let's face it, if a God or a beer could be *proven* to have the ability to reach the parts no other could, the promoter (in this case you) would be rendered redundant.

If this hypothetical debate were then to concentrate on life *before* death, the odds would surely fall heavily in my favour. If you are right and there is a Saviour, then I would hope he would be broadminded enough to see fit to forgive me and welcome me into the Kingdom of Heaven, just as you tell us he would. On the other hand, if you are wrong, isn't it just a little scandalous the way you use psychological blackmail against those pathetic fellow beings who look to you for guidance. You tell them how bad they are, encourage them to have sins to confess on a Sunday but reassure that by living a worthy, God-fearing life all will be well. So, riddled with feelings of guilt and inadequacy, the congregation kneels before Him, prepared to accept His wrath, never questioning. Must people deny themselves many of life's pleasures in order that they may be acceptable to God? Does the end justify the means? I feel it is on a par with the government using taxes from tobacco to fund the health service.

For many years now I have believed that this is the one and

only chance at life, and we must make the most of it. I tend to
think I have the more positive and realistic approach.

I would suggest it could only be to the good of mankind for you
to ponder on my note. I don't expect you will be overcome by a
radical change of heart, but perhaps one day you might find some
truth in what I say, sit up with a sudden sense of realization,
laugh at the doom and gloom you have spread in the past, live for
the present instead of the future and as that well-known slogan
goes ... CHOOSE LIFE!

> Yours sincerely,
> MRS ANGRY!
>
> (Barbara Thompson)

DEAR BOB GELDOF
AND OTHER FAMOUS PEOPLE...

Dear God,

Well, here we are! I said I'd write to you, didn't I? One of these days; when the time was right; when I felt I was ready.

Well, I think I'm ready now.

I'm not sure what to say or how to say it. I mean, you must be tired of letters asking for good health, miracles and large fortunes? I can imagine all the greedy little believers, scribbling away, praying that their secret desires will reach you the next morning by first class or air-mail.

It's not a very nice job you have, is it? Sitting there wondering who to help or who not to. I mean, all those millions begging for food or peace or a job. It's just not fair, is it? I bet you could do with some help? I suppose you could cause an earthquake or two, or a flood. That way you'd perhaps cause some believers to enter your factory and give you a hand so to speak. Then again, I can imagine the disasters would only create more work in the long run. It's a bit of a vicious circle, isn't it? Perhaps you don't need any help anyway, although it has been said that you don't do a thing.

Now don't get me wrong! I'm not trying to imply that you're lazy, or that you don't help people. Far from it! I know that you do. Only the other day my next-door neighbour told me how she nearly walked in front of a bus. She swears blind that a voice told her to stop. Just in time, she said, one more step and that would have been it! Said someone must have been watching over her. Well, we know who that someone is, don't we? I mean, the amount of poor souls your angels must have saved when you think about it! It must be staggering! Still, I bet even they get a

117

bit fed up having to save every Tom, Dick and Hilda that asks for it? I mean, you do help everyone, don't you? Well, the vicar, the priest and other members of the cloth I've met, have always insisted that you do. Not directly or so obviously of course; in more of a roundabout way. But still, you do help.

Ever thought of taking a holiday? You could send lightning bolts from out of the blue, throw in the deep resounding voice, and hey presto! A million, billion souls shaking in their vanity-ridden shoes. Tell them you're off, going away for a few centuries. Say you won't bother sending a postcard: you'll probably be back before it arrives.

Then again, I was just thinking! Perhaps you're already on holiday? How would one know? If so, who the Hell's reading this letter? (Oops! Excuse the Hades bit!) If it's not God reading this letter, will the reader kindly pass it on!

I know I've been rabbiting on somewhat, and that I should get to the point. But the thing is, I need a little help. No! No! It's not health or miracles I require: I'm feeling fine. No, what I require, or I should say, what I'd like if possible, is not so much a large fortune or wealth, but more a little bit of help in obtaining it.

I think I am acquiring the ability and skill to obtain the wealth that I desire (which I assure you is not astronomical) but the fact is, it's taking too long. I need a little nudge, just a little one, to help me along. Say a thousand or a five-thousand one. Yes, I'm referring to pounds of course, money pounds. British Sterling!

You see, I have this feeling I can write. Stories, plays, poetry, that sort of thing. I've had lots of letters admiring my work, praising my efforts (especially competition-wise) or telling me how clever they think I am and how the reader or editor looks forward to reading my next manuscript. But the trouble is, I don't feel as though I'm improving! I have nothing to show for it! Well, apart from dusty letters, tatty magazines and yellowed newspaper clippings. What I really want, is a big win. A prize! Something to remember! Something I can always look back on and say, there, that's when my life began to change; when it all came together; when I really began to work.

The rewards are there, I know. I've been told it so often. I can even see them myself at times, although mostly distant or in my dreams. But they are there, I have to be patient and wait my turn. But it's so bloody hard! There seems to be no end of others popping up and taking their share. I feel as though I won't be around long enough to take mine. I'll end up becoming one of those unlucky buggers that dies before anyone spots their talent.

I don't want that to happen to me! But if it must, then one, one prize. Cash or otherwise, it doesn't really matter, just as long as it's big. So please, just one! I'll never write to you again, I promise.

I suppose this letter will be filed under the 'Greedy Little Bastards' section or the 'Greedy, Impatient and Extremely Selfish' one. But that's the chance I have to take. I have to try! I can't help myself! Please help me!

I look forward to your reply.

Yours sincerely (and faithfully),
John Walsh

Dear Mr Geldof,

Suddenly, on Wednesday last, Carole the Capitalist was born. It happened without prior warning in Fortnum and Mason's – in the Food Hall, to be exact. A glimpse of hand-made chocolates, fancily jarred preserves, conserves and jams was enough to dispel utterly any long-held Socialist tendencies I may have owned to before entering this gourmands' Nirvana and to admit me to the 'Let them eat cake!' brigade (and preferably Black Forest Gateau at that).

Without the slightest twinge your humble narrator, impoverished Student Intellectual, found herself as if in a dream, handing over an impossible sum for the tiniest gold box emblazoned with the legend 'Fortnum and Mason' and containing enough of their hand-made chocolates (probably put together by starving orphans in a garret in Stepney) to feed a surfeited sparrow for perhaps 10 seconds. I passed on dreamily through the rest of the Food Hall, bearing the little bag with my purchase aloft – my membership of this exclusive club proclaimed. Next, came the tentative hand in the handbag as the cheque-book was searched for – a passport to even more luxury goodies – French cheeses lovingly mused over with all the earnestness attached to researching a Ph.D. China teas, honeys gained from expeditions to Peruvian peaks (where the specially bred Fortnum and Mason bees make their hives), exquisite shortbreads from a highland-crofted, ruddy-cheeked Scottish granny's kitchen, the most Gallic-looking of French mustards...

But, Bob, I digress. Having somehow forced myself out of this Olympus, this Holy Grail of the seekers-after-luxury (and foreign tourists), I stepped out into Piccadilly and shook off its awesome spell, like Orpheus stepping out of the Underworld, blinking in the sunlight. I took a deep breath. I had escaped (relatively) unscathed, apart from the noticeable dent in my wallet (and conscience) made by those chocs. I still had my tube fare home, however, so counted myself lucky. It could have been worse, much worse, I mused, as I walked along Piccadilly, head down to avoid tantalizing shop windows. A tiny *frisson* of horror shivered up and down my body as I thought on those hapless souls forever condemned to walk those hallowed halls, cooing delightedly over those beautifully packaged containers of sauce tartare...

Luxury (as I am sure you well know) is an easy habit to acquire and a hard one to break. It resides as much in high-class Food Halls as in Cartier's or Zandra Rhodes' dressing rooms, except that in Food Halls it all seems a bit more innocent somehow, doesn't it? It is only food, after all, and food is necessary for survival, isn't it? One can even manage to justify a fridge full of paté de fois gras on that rationalization. It's all a bit like the compulsive gambler who tells himself that fruit machines are just a harmless bit of fun. The principle is what is important here, and the Luxury, or Pleasure Principle is one which is as potentially damaging to mankind's mental health as alcohol or drug abuse is to physical health.

Since the war years, the masses have been allowed, indeed encouraged, by the insidious serpent's voice of advertising to indulge in luxuries, that is, in what is surplus to their everyday living requirements. At first glance this looks fine to the Socialist or egalitarian – why shouldn't the worker partake of the fruits of his labour in the same way as his master, after all? What bothers me (and obviously you too, Bob) is the question of whether or not it is really morally viable for the Western masses to enjoy so much that is surplus to everyday needs while the Third World – our Twilight Zone – starves?

As far as I can see, the time for Western complacency has come to an end. Our high living standard must be ameliorated somewhat to allow us to extend our surpluses to our less fortunate world brethren – this is the responsibility of both our governments and ourselves. To allow ourselves to be manipulated by advertising men into thinking that only the right car, fitted kitchen, clothes, cosmetics or brand of alcohol can make our lives worth living is surely a crime against the rest of suffering humanity. Perhaps the time has arrived for us to review our 'needs' and to give a thought to what really constitutes our daily bread, and appreciate that everything above that is luxury.

All that remains for me to say in this letter is here is my cheque for Live Aid, and with it my admiration and thanks for your efforts in stirring up such an overwhelming response to your famine appeal.

Yours sincerely,
Carole Farnan

Dear Superwoman,

It is just not fair that you can make everything seem to be so
easy. I mean, of course, all the superb articles that I devour,
which relate to making the best use of one's time, energy,
intelligence, opportunities, skills, etc.

How do all the women like yourself, manage to make such a
success of their lifestyles? Don't get me wrong, it's not that I
disbelieve a word of it, on the contrary, I am filled with
admiration at such enterprising groups, if not a little envious at
the fact that I haven't managed to do anything that is out of the
ordinary, or even succeeded in doing any one thing so perfectly
that I could say it would be remembered.

It seems that although I dream of being an efficient and well
organized person, completely in control of any situation that may
arise, the truth is, they remain dreams.

No, I would appear to fall into the category of a 'Wendy Craig',
the good intentions are there, but never really seem to bear fruit.
What am I doing wrong? It is all crystal clear at the outset, the
theory seems to be perfect, but the practice is another matter. Not
enough time, not enough money, not enough space, are they
really all just excuses, I'm sure they must be, but I refuse to give
in to the idea that it is just me. Something does nevertheless seem
always to get in the way. So I tell myself that the idea was wrong,
not really the right thing for me, all I need to do is find out what I
am exceptionally good at; unfortunately the answer to that does
not come readily. You see I am interested in all sorts of things,
but not dedicated to any single one in particular. Huh, fickle
woman you may think. Perhaps – but still the feeling remains,
that there is something special hidden inside me, if only I could
find it.

I wonder if any of you Superwomen who manage to run a
successful business, be it a cottage industry or otherwise, whilst
running a home and children, and still finding time to entertain,
have ever been doubtful about your own capabilities. Did you
ever make sponge cakes that insist on sinking in the middle like
mine always do? Did you realize that the only way to get ahead
and on top of the daily routine was to get up at least two hours
earlier in the morning, only to resent getting out of a warm bed

when the alarm went off, turn over instead and resolve definitely to start tomorrow. Perhaps not.

Maybe I secretly rather like my slightly chaotic, always hectic lifestyle, otherwise why on earth do I put up with it? On the other hand, it is possible that I loathe it so much that I am always trying to change it, which doesn't help at all really; I only end up loathing myself for not being one thing or another – back to square one.

Even now as I write in the supposed privacy of my bedroom, ignoring the noise of the TV from outside the door, worn out from a full day's work outside the home, followed by cooking and housework for a family of five, and suppressing my guilt at not having done the ironing, even now my poor neglected husband comes to ask 'what are you doing in there' (he is used to my company whilst he is engaged in TV viewing). Might as well go to bed, he says, looking very sorry for himself. Guilty feelings rise up again, so I prepare for bed also. Bathroom first for the nightly routine of cleanse, tone and moisturize, grabbing pen and paper on the way to write a bit more, making it all seem so furtive somehow. But not for long, eldest son requests that I hurry up as he needs to use the loo.

How about a revival of the old-fashioned household where Mother ruled supreme in her Castle, baked cakes and steamed puddings, plenty of time to polish the furniture until you could see your face in it, sheets starched and crisp like they are in some hotels still, roaring open fire to greet the family on a winter's eve and a table set out properly for mealtimes instead of a plate on one's lap in front of the TV. Not for her the pressure of Superwoman staring back from the screen in her Space Age Kitchen.

Oh yes, we've come a long way, the benefits for woman have been immense you know, it's just that I am finding it extremely difficult to strike a happy medium, if there is one. Well, you can't have your cake and eat it say the Old Wives, but couldn't I just have a nibble, get some idea of what it tastes like. That of course is where the problem lies, because I fear that is precisely what I am doing, and having nibbled I think I want some more, but don't quite know whether I can manage it all.

Was it really Eve who tempted Adam with the Apple, or did he eat the whole lot, leaving us to wonder ever after what on earth it tasted like, determined that one day we would have our own Bitter-Sweet Apple to chew on.

Well Superwoman, having actually managed to finish writing this letter to you, and finding the time – sorry, organized the time – to set it out in print, my thanks to you for diverting my attention and spurring me into action. You have been my shoulder to cry on, I hope you don't mind.

I remain an admirer of you in all you do, good luck and best wishes.

Kind regards,
Theresa Flynn

Dear Life...

I thought of you today. I always do whenever I look out of my
window. The big copper beech tree opposite brings you to mind
again and again. It's been there since I moved into this basement
flat nine months ago, waving its terraced branches, whispering,
filling my window with its leaves. The sunlight penetrates them
sometimes, transforming the olive greens, reds and dark
chestnuts into a radiant mosaic umbrella overhead.

It's been a long time since you and I first met. I don't
remember the very early times but I've seen the photographs –
black and white images of my parents and their friends, perched
on cliff-tops and beaches in Cornwall after the war. My father has
the collar of his heavy Polish Air Force greatcoat up against the
wind; my mother, smiling a young smile, kneels to hold me
upright for the camera. I look like a tiny, puzzled scarecrow.

Those were hard days for that company of refugees, you had
given them a battering. But its survivors only tell how you
brought camaraderie and humour into the leaking Nissen huts,
the Christmas dinners for thirteen cooked impossibly over a
one-ringed stove. They accepted the austerity with which you
painted the post-war years. After all, you were Polish too, or so it
seemed.

Later, I do remember you being there as I put on my new
school uniform and took my first steps, on crisp mornings, out
into the world. I was a hopeful child, quite innocent and eager to
learn. To begin with, anyway. Instantly captivated by the
wonderfully strange sounds I'd heard, I approached a teacher at
the end of class. Please say something again in French I said
before retreating, punctured by her embarrassment and scorn-
filled eyes.

It couldn't work. I never found a way to succeed is that
over-rarified, academic atmosphere, and in the struggle to
maintain some kind of self-esteem, I resorted, finally, to war. My
school reports made this abundantly public, deepening my
father's disappointment and my lonely guilt. Those dusty
spinsters with their double-barrelled names and narrow lives were
not impressed by my attempts to gain attention, especially when
these took the form of certain graffiti effects, not without talent,

that I carried out on the hitherto-revered and graceful statuette that stood outside the headmistress's room.

All that changed in the '60s though. You seemed to undergo a transformation after I took that coveted place in Art School. The sound of The Doors drifted out of my open windows that first summer I spent in London and something changed the first moment I heard Bob Dylan sing – the cracked, fractured voice pentrated everything – involved, uncompromising, ironic.

You were very West Coast then, wearing beads and velvet and going to San Francisco. You seemed especially present, perhaps because I was beginning to experience you in such an intensely visual way. The ultramarine and gold I chose to paint my room, the violet-blue shadows beneath pearly plates of oranges on a blue-check cloth (a tea-time by Bonnard), the pearly-soft rainbow stripes iridescing on an inky Mexican shawl, the violently hot pinks and cobalt blues and parrot greens I loved seeing scorched into black backgrounds, all these sensations crystallized into a life-long, obsessive and hungry love for colour.

At the same time, I'm ashamed to say that I took you for granted completely. In some subtly arrogant way, I believed that you belonged only to me and a select circle of friends. I thought only other people would become old. I thought I was special.

Well, you put paid to some of these golden and naive illusions in 1966, the year my father died.

I had survived my mother's frequent departures into sickness, the often scary visits to the 'madhouse' as she chose to call it, but this was different. My father wasn't coming back. And the hardest thing of all was trying to understand why, when I left the hospital on the morning of his death, nothing *else* had changed. Clouds continued moving overhead, traffic continued in the street. You hadn't even noticed.

I had you blacklisted for a while after that but I couldn't keep it up for long. Too much kept happening, kept being offered. Like the scholarship that allowed me to travel in America, coast-to-coast, in 1971. I loved everything about it, the generosity, brashness, confidence, pace. I loved the sense of anything being possible, the glittering beauty of neon in cities at night, the bold deserts, the friendliness of strangers, the food. And I felt at home for the first time, a foreigner abroad in a nation of foreigners.

When I returned, I was engaged and I got married. It wasn't

the best decision I'd ever made, but I didn't get your message until five years later and, by then, my marriage had become an uneasy contract that might have gone on for ever if certain qualities, long asleep, had not begun to stir and reassert themselves.

These fuelled the journey through the next ten years, via psychotherapy and divorce; arriving at dead-ends on the outside and discovering secret passages on the inside; propelling me towards today. Thanks for being there, constant and persuasive, while I turned my attention, finally, to myself, discovering (to your gentle amusement) not a devoted daughter...model wife ...successful careerist, emigré artist or best friend...but someone else. Someone less than perfect yet more loveable than I'd imagined.

Life...I won't ask you about the future or the secrets you still have hidden up your sleeve. You'll smile that enigmatic smile again and with the same seductive charm, turn the conversation to the autumn light outside, the larkspur dropping its soft petals now, the copper beech tree opposite, the ebb and flow of seasons, feelings, friendships...

What can I do...but listen?

A.C.

To: Mr Henry Ford – whereabouts unknown,

It's got to be said. It's been on my mind for years. A little thing like your being dead won't stop me, Henry. There's nothing I write that I wouldn't be prepared to say to your face, if you still had one. Because, Henry, you stand in my dock accused of inflicting upon us that most successful and loathsome of inventions, the motor car.

Oh don't worry, Henry, you're in no danger. I can hear your legions of supporters already, baying for my oil. I accept that I'm in a miniscule minority. I appreciate that when people tell me they couldn't possibly manage without their wheels they really believe it. It speaks volumes about what we've become.

The truth is that the motor car is responsible for the ruination of the countryside, the destruction of the character of countless British towns, the pollution of the environment and the shattering of peace and quiet. The motor car has made the ordinary mortal lazy, impatient and dangerous. It ranks with cancer and heart disease as a major killer, and contributes hugely to both. It has changed the whole face of Britain, indisputably for the worse; it has ripped out its heart.

I'm aware, Henry, that in a society where the motor car is idolized like a little tin god these views put me on a par with members of the Flat Earth Society. I know I'm branded as an eccentric escapist perched at my loom thinking up new recipes for lentils and foaming at the mouth when my neighbour tells me she uses an aerosol flykiller. It's a bit like carnivores regarding vegetarians as cranks. So convinced are they that meat is essential they see anyone who spurns it in favour of the noodle as deranged. Car drivers are the same. When I refuse a colleague's kind offer of a lift because I prefer to walk the mile home his expression is one of such horror it seems I've told him I'll be carrying a hippo up the road. 'My Angela couldn't possibly carry all that shopping home,' he says. Since the pound of sprouts and box of Daz Automatic in my basket are hardly likely to dislocate my clavicle, I imagine his Angela must be a tiny, frail, wan little thing smiling though the pain. Quite a shock when she turns out to be a twelve-stone hammer thrower for Stoke.

It is because of the car that multitudes of British people get virtually no exercise, succumbing to heart attacks and arthritis and ending up on the Intensive Care Unit, costing us a bomb in Get Well cards and fruit. And when you get into town to purchase these delicacies for the invalid, can you honestly say for sure which town you're in? Today they all look exactly the same. Same shopping precinct with the same stores, same supermarkets, same multi-storey car parks, same ring roads. And, of course, the same motorways. I wonder, Henry, how many animal lives and habitats have been destroyed by highways and motorways, all for the car? I wonder why we assume we're entitled to treat fellow species with such arrogance when they've just as much right to a decent life on this planet as ourselves? And human animals fare little better. Predictably, Henry, modern towns are planned by motorists for motorists. It takes a military manoeuvre to get from one side of some roads to the other. It helps if you're a potential suicide. Of course if you're a whippet or an Olympic sprinter you're well away but anybody slightly less spry is in trouble. And don't assume that all drivers will stop to make sure you're still breathing, Henry – that might cause them to lose a second. It is ironic that at a time when we can get from A to B faster than ever before people are more impatient and bad-tempered with delay than ever. It is not simply that we have no time to stand and stare – we've forgotten how to. The other day I offended a neighbour of mine by not knowing what sort his new car was. Well sorry, Henry, but I can't tell a Cavalier from a Roundhead or a Maxi from a taxi. Give me a horse and cart any day.

'They all look the same to me,' I say in tones I hope are acid. 'Biscuit tins on wheels.'

He couldn't have been more insulted if I'd told him I'd seen his mother soliciting on the bowling green.

Another neighbour of mine. Came home the other day, supported by friends, distraught, voice quaking with emotion. What had happened? Wife raped? Lost his job? Son run off with a weightlifter? No. Another motorist had run into the back of his own pride and joy, putting it temporarily off the road. That he himself was unharmed was not regarded as something to be thankful for. The claim that we take better care of our cars than ourselves is perfectly true.

The car is gradually taking over, Henry. Tearing up the countryside, replacing it with endless highways and car parks, poisoning the air with fumes and noise, killing and maiming, blocking the horizon with one monumental traffic jam. What a pity you're dead, Henry. You ought to be hung.

Yours truly,
Gillian Lewis

Dear D.M. Thomas,

Am I a swallow or a budgerigar, one wonders? Perhaps if we
meet, I shall find out. I've just finished your beautiful novel,
Swallow, and have read all the others, including your poetry (ah,
your poetry!) and felt I must write to you. Then you gave me very
great pleasure on a radio programme of that name when you chose
so many of the prose and poetry pieces that I myself would have
chosen. So many of my favourites! Yeats, Joyce,
Pushkin... Sexton. We have so much in common.

How I should love to meet the man (so rare) who understands –
or feels – what a woman is! I shall put a flower in my hair like the
Andalusian girls and drive through darkness to your greyfriar's
cottage, if you agree. Yes I will.

Are you wondering why I have your home address? We met
twice before. You autographed *The White Hotel* (in black ink,
alas!) and included your address, saying perhaps one day we
would meet again to discuss the imaginative intensity that makes
poetry, makes life. Shall I come to Hereford! Yes yes I will.

I have been dreaming in bronze during these warm autumnal
days, rehearsing this letter. Like Bellow's Herzog, I've written
dozens of letters to you, none of which I've had the 'chutspah' to
send. But this one, I will. Yes yes I will.

But if you reply, shall I come to you, bronzed and rested from
my Adriatic tryst? Or will I write saying I cannot come, won't
come. And then drive up through darkness, arriving breathless
and trembling. Then ask you with my eyes to ask me again. Yes
yes I will Yes.

> A sister swallow?
> Marianne Nault

PS If all else fails, I shall meet you at the *Cosmo* Book Day. If not,
I shall send another letter, written under the statue of the Bronze
Horseman, Pushkin, in Moscow.

Dear Nigel Lawson,

This is a plea from the heart – and lungs! I am desperate for you to raise the tax on cigarettes so I can no longer afford to smoke.

I realize that the tax is fixed so that taking into consideration the law of diminishing returns sufficient people still smoke, enabling you to run the country's economy on the revenue raised. Surely, you could raise the tax so high – for example making a packet of twenty cost between £5 and £6 – that cigarettes will still be bought by those rich and hooked enough to spend the money. Cigarettes will thus become a status symbol, smoked in luxurious dining rooms over the brandy and liqueurs; so revenue will still be raised from their sale.

But people like me – poorish and hooked, will be saved from killing themselves.

Dear Mr Lawson – have *you* ever tried to give up smoking? I am the world's expert at it – I have done it hundreds of times.

Take this morning (I smoked my nth 'last one' at midnight last night) – at 7.30 a.m. I received a phone bill that should pay for another nice shiny yellow van for BT, and ET I reckon has been using my phone – and not a cigarette in the house. At 8 a.m. the cat brought up the innards of her night's hunting expedition on the hall carpet – I want a fag! At 8.15 a.m. one son accused me of letting another finish up the last of the Rice Krispies, 'there's no food in this house!' (I don't want *food* – I just want a cigarette.) At 8.40 a.m. I started a search for a vital rugby boot. I lifted up a fishing rod that was on top of a pile of junk. It became caught on Action Man's tank then flew up, hit me in the mouth and chipped my front tooth. Rugby boot found outside the back door, covered in mud and soaked by the rain. 9.10 a.m. I left the house in a state of near undress, my nerves shredded to pieces and headed for the nearest fag shop.

My every attempt is like that – have you a heart, Mr Lawson? I'm killing myself off at a rate of knots – my chest hurts – every day at some point I'm convinced I have lung cancer – the frantic, heart-stopping panic makes me reach for a cigarette.

Only if I cannot possible afford to smoke will I stop. It's a revolting habit, I agree – but lovely too. So comforting. When my self-esteem is low I need to smoke. My self-esteem is always low – I am one of your average females. So, please help me, although I suppose you've chucked this letter by now.

Dear Waste Paper Bin, have you ever got home, exhausted, to find the place looks like the aftermath of a particularly nasty push on the Somme and then people are making *demands* on you; on your time, attention and emotions? The only comfort is a cigarette – the only thing that makes life bearable. The smoke fogs up nasty, bright reality all around you. OK so if you light up you're in bother but for the rest of us who aren't waste paper baskets it's heavenly solace, a wonderful ten-minute hibernation.

If I become ill from smoking who will care for my children? The sorrow and misery will be incalculable. Is that why the Chancellor doesn't care enough to raise the tax or even ban them? Is he only into items that can be calculated, added up and balanced out at the end of the day? People's lives aren't like that – not black and white and divisible by 10.

What's happened to our caring society? Does no one in that grey-suited governing gang care about the human suffering caused by smoking? OK I should stop smoking – an end to worry, ill-health and financial crises but I *can't*. I can't help myself and there must be thousands like me – I'm sure in that office you know the figures – they're related to every lovely big cheque you receive from the tobacco companies.

I'd write to Sir Walter Raleigh and tell him he was a pratt if he wasn't dead and the GPO are bad enough at delivering letters to the living.

Now this letter is getting disorganized – because I'm upset – hang on, I'll light a cigarette so I stop being uptight.

That's better, where was I? Yes, writing a useless letter, part of a wasted life. I tell myself every day that life's not a rehearsal, it's the main picture and I'm putting it out of focus with every fag I light.

I think I'll now be off to make myself a cup of coffee to have with this cigarette; mind you, I'll have finished it by the time the kettle boils so I'll have to have another one to go with the coffee ...

Yours faithfully
(I lie, I'm SDP),
Kate Harkness

Dear Father Christmas,

I realize I'm being somewhat premature in issuing you with my list of wants for this Yuletide but I do not want a repeat performance of last year's miserable turn-out.

When I listed 'sexy lingerie' I had hoped for something more erotic than what I actually got! I realize I'm rather bulbous in shape but that suspender belt didn't even fit as a garter. The veins on my leg looked like a map of England and I kept passing out. And as for anything peep-holed the nearest I got was a pair of moth-eaten bed socks from Auntie May. I'd hoped for more than my big toe to protrude! That tube of magic love cream did nothing for my sex life either but I have to admit it did wonders for piles.

So I'm hoping for a much better show this year to make up for last year's disappointment.

Incidentally on this list I've written a new car. This does not mean a dinky toy as you so wittingly provided last year. It might be more economical but its hardly likely to impress the girls down at the local slimming club. Which brings me to another point. I know you are only being polite when you buy me everything in a size 10 but the girls in Marks & Sparks are beginning to snigger when I have my annual trek in January to swap my pressies for size 16s.

I do understand how your job is becoming harder each year, what with the economic climate being what it is and the installation of central heating – not to mention the rising cost of stabling the reindeer for a whole year when they only work for one day out of 365.

Have you ever thought about a time-and-motion study. I'm sure you could save yourself a fortune if you were to sit down and think about it. You could automate the reindeer and move your factory to Milton Keynes – and what about delivering the pressies at the end of January? It would give you a chance to snap up a few bargains in the sales.

134

Anyway, I sincerely hope I fare better this year but I've given you more time to get your act together this time.

Love from Christine (aged 28½)

PS Don't forget my holiday to Sri Lanka.

(Christine Edmonds)

DEAR *COSMO*

Dear *Cosmo,*

Attempt number three to write a letter. Stupid really. I have always written long, chatty and hopefully amusing letters in the past but I took your competition very seriously.

It was last week and I was feeling about as low as one can get when I reached the competition in your magazine. I sat and wrote a letter I have always wanted to write about a doctor who let out that I have MS when told not to. It was a long, unhappy letter and I posted it. Did I feel a fool when I got a bit further on and found an article all about 'Mother Courage'? Couldn't let my letter go even if it was from the heart, etc.

But: how do you get a letter out of a box that is standard Post Office sealed? You can't I thought. It's midnight by now and I am now worrying about two things. How to get the letter back and why the hell did I put real names in it?

At one o'clock, somewhat scantyly (that isn't spelt right) clad, I am writing letter number two to your competition. Shorter than number one it pleaded for you to put the first one in a dustbin. I go to bed and dream of angry faceless doctors chasing me with rolled-up copies of *Cosmo.*

I do not give up even if I worry a lot, so got up very early, drove to the letter box with the dread letter in it and sat in the car and waited for the postman. Knowing they are not allowed to give back letters didn't help. He arrived thirty minutes late by which time I had another worry. Will I be late for work – no one would believe I could be late because I was sitting at a letter box waiting to get a letter to a competition back, would you? He arrived, an officious, small, plump man. I was most surprised when I did not get a lecture on the sanctity of a letter box. He demanded proof of identity and handwriting. I dashed to the car to get both. He meanwhile was hurriedly shovelling letters into his sack, but too late – I spotted mine half out of the box and not in the sack. I think he felt he had a forty-year-old human mosquito for company by this time and on having me shove my ID card behind his glasses more or less he gave up and I went off triumphantly clutching my letter.

If you want a cure for feeling down get a letter back you should never have posted in the first place.

I tore it up but being a little bit on the mean side (or trying to save trees if you look at it that way which sounds better) I saved the envelope. Shot off to work and bounced with enthusiasm all over everyone. Not on a Monday morning, not a good idea at all. Try *not* explaining why you haven't got Monday blues.

Then when I got home I thought why waste the envelope, don't steam off the stamp, tell *Cosmo* that they help one out of the miserys in the most unusual ways. I felt better for writing the first letter as it really let off steam and then I stopped worrying about not getting the job I wanted and the last of my family leaving London to live in the West Country and the MS making me so clumsy, and worried about the letter instead. Bang your head on a wall to take the pain from somewhere else principle.

Now I'm back to my normal optimistic self. Of course it hasn't answered the basic questions 'when will I learn to live with MS' and 'why did the rat of a doctor in Central London tell me'. I'll never forget being on my own standing on the pavement on a bright, sunny, crisp morning staring at the blue sky and thinking 'why me'? I went and spent nearly £20 in Neal's Yard wholefoods shop, I suppose on the principle that good food might help!!

Now I'm chatting again and I really ought to leave for work so will stop. Thank you for curing 'the miserys' or is it 'miseries'. (That looks wrong).

> Yours sincerely,
> Jacqueline D. F. Murray

Take a letter, Miss Smith. Or are you perhaps Mrs Smith, one of the thousands of that name who because of a silly old joke are still embarrassed when they and their husbands book in at hotels for a weekend break? I don't know you well enough to call you Marcelle, which, if you'll forgive me mentioning it, is a name that recalls a permanent wave of long ago.

Or maybe you were named after Marcel Proust, and if you enjoy such literary name-dropping I have to point out that *I* bear the name of Dorothy Parker's husband. I suspect that more people have enjoyed reading *Babbitt* than have ever got through all the volumes of *A la Recherche* of something or other. Pardon my French, but there does seem to be a strong Gallic influence in *Cosmo* – all those adverts for perfumes, some in French so advanced that it is beyond many of your readers. Moi, I never could understand the subjunctive.

If it were not open to misunderstanding, I would suggest *Cosmo* should have a section on French Life and Letters. It might answer a question that's long puzzled me – what is the French for Male Chauvinist Pig, the original Monsieur Chauvin having been a Frenchman.

Forgive my musings, but *Cosmo* does encourage such pseudo-intellectual ideas, with its articles on polytechnics this month and a section for new undergraduates promised for next time. One would think it was trying to imitate its elder sister, *She* who is above criticism. But *Cosmo* is slightly more down-market (an expression I hate, but I think you know what I mean) and part of it caters for working women. A friend in the Special Branch thinks it must be a front for the lefties, with those articles attacking the Government over sweatshops and crèches and unfair dismissal. Maggie will not be pleased.

Talking of front organizations, what exactly is the Letter Writing Bureau? Are the notepaper and envelope manufacturers behind it, or is it Post Office public relations trying to encourage us to buy more stamps? I've been suspicious of the postal authorities ever since they dropped the General from the Post Office, so that nowadays you see postpersons carrying sacks with the initials PO on them, which I think is rather rude.

Something else that is not often discussed in polite society, at least not in my half of the world. *Cosmo* does seem to have an enormous number of adverts for tampons. The only reason for mentioning this is that it's given me a spiffing idea for winning the next General Election. If you promise not to pass it on I'll tell you. Agreed?

A large number of voters are women. So all that is required is for one of the parties to announce that it intends to abolish VAT on these apparently necessary items, and the swingometer will swerve accordingly. After the election the winners could always put a tax on baby food to make up for the loss of revenue. You think I'm joking? Remember, income tax was supposed to be temporary.

You may be wondering what a nice man like me is doing in a competition like this, or why I should be looking at *Cosmo* at all. It's brought home by one of our daughters, who wanted to go in for the competition herself. The presumption of youth, indeed. I said her mother and I needed a holiday more than she does, and even offered to pay her 80p for the magazine. So she may still be having a go on her own, and the best of luck, etc.

But what really encouraged me were the kind words by your astrological correspondent about the wonderful opportunities facing members of the Aries clan. As a male I ought to be distrustful of any astrologer called Circe, but when she dollops out the flattery how can I resist.

It's handy, too, to blame the stars for what Shakespeare called my goatish disposition. Incidentally, I'm sceptical of Tom Crabtree's figures about adultery. It's not the sort of question people give an honest reply to. When I look around my colleagues or the passengers on a bus I refuse to believe it. Perhaps I'm naive.

However, being a Ram my natural habitat is the mountains, which explains where this letter is coming from. If you were working for the *Tatler* I might have suggested St Moritz, a few miles away, but it's not really our style, and this particular place is well supplied with easy footpaths for walkers of all ages.

Finally, a little grumble (what would life be without them?) Why should women get a pension at 60 while we men have to soldier on, assuming we have a job, until 65? Unfair, unfair, I cry. But never mind. Thanks to this holiday I look at the world, and Cosmokind, with a more cheerful eye.

S. L. Short

Dear *Cosmopolitan*,

This is the letter I've been dreaming of writing for several months now. I find it difficult to comprehend that I am actually in the position to write and thank *Cosmopolitan* for making my dream come true – in awarding me winner of your September competition. I shall never again find myself debating over whether or not I can afford the price of *Cosmopolitan*, this has put a whole new perspective on life. The times I have glanced at competitions and have felt disappointed when after perusing one sees the familiar phrase 'and then complete the sentence in not more than twenty words...' After a few minutes of toying with different word combinations, making vain and futile attempts to be witty or humorous, I have resigned myself to the fact that there goes another competition I shan't win because I haven't entered! – pretty logical. I am also grateful that I didn't have to match A's outfit with C's profession or complete a cryptic crossword or consider the attributes of X and place into appropriate boxes in order of importance.

I haven't written a letter now since the one that won me the competition. I have been too busy packing and preparing myself for this exciting trip to Peru. I felt it my duty to put pen to paper – I could not just telephone, besides from Peru the cost would be extortionate and I would be bound to leave something out. Sitting here on the plane I only wish I hadn't forgotten to pack my personalized stationery. Anyway letter writing is a wonderful way to keep oneself occupied during long flights!

This is the letter that marks an enormous change in my life for who could have thought it feasible that one letter written in England could have led me to the country of my dreams – what an opportunity! All I can say is thank goodness for letters – what a wonderful innovation and of course thanks for competitions and thanks to *Cosmopolitan* – not forgetting the Royal Mail – the wonderful institution that has made letter writing and competition winning possible. All things considered I think this letter could qualify as a 'thank you' letter. I might have sent a thank you card but that wouldn't have sufficed. Instead I have written a letter to equal the one I wrote for the competition.

You couldn't imagine how thrilled I was to see the letter on the mat with the *Cosmopolitan* stamp visible on the envelope. This was the most eagerly anticipated letter than I have waited for. I had purposely tried to put all thoughts of ever winning out of mind to avoid disappointment.

The letter that won me this fantastic holiday was certainly the subject of much procrastination – should I – shouldn't I – what on earth could I choose to write about – but on reflection it was a really cool move. I made sure I took time to write my letter so that I at least had the opportunity and excitement of the possibility of a very special letter coming through my door.

I think when one is writing a letter one should certainly say it all and not hold back. I can say that I think I deserved to win this competition – so what's wrong with a little modesty? – Someone had to win and it just happened to be me for a change and I no longer have a chip on my shoulder. To give me credit I can say that I was particularly eligible because I exceeded the average number of letters written by someone of my age group in a year by approximately ten letters – so there!

How I hated writing letters at school – for English exams – was it 'yours faithfully' or 'yours sincerely' and where on earth did the date go – was it the left or the right hand side? Still it looks as if my education has stood me in good stead! Hopefully everything is in the correct tense and legible now that I have won the competition and am reviewing the situation that led to this streak of good luck.

One also recalls the thank you letters one has felt obliged to write after each birthday – I thought birthdays were pleasurable – that's life I guess! If one failed to write those perfunctory little notes one was always reminded by one's parents. 'Well if you don't write, don't expect to be remembered next year! – enough to get anyone involved in industrious sessions of letter writing – what a shame they didn't have photo-copiers in those days! No seriously when one gets started it's not so bad but it's all too easy to put it off until tomorrow, until so many tomorrows have passed that one is seriously worried if one's friends and relations could be doubting one's existence. To be honest I have been brought up to see letters as an integral part of life – never shall I forget those compulsory Sunday letter routines at boarding school, after church, where each and every boarder was forced to produce a letter and until it was safely marked off was not excused to do better things (if that was at all possible at boarding school!) I had to suffer the double penalty of having to write two as my parents were unfortunately separated. But of course this letter is of my own free will – and for no gain?! – unlike the letter I wrote for the competition when my friend whom I promised to take with me was offering words of encouragement or should we say threats?

Of course I must add in case I haven't painted too rosy a picture of letter writing that it can be a real pleasure. Perhaps it's the anticipation of the return letter that spurs one on to write to old friends and relations. At least one's parents don't fret about the telephone bill.

Well I'm running out of valuable time – the seat-belt lights are illuminated, so I must say 'Thanks a million *Cosmopolitan*' – and I'll write again.

Miss S. L. E. Powell

Dearest *Cosmo*,

I hope you will allow me to call you that. *Cosmopolitan* is such a beautiful name (Italian, I suppose, like the ice-cream), but I feel I know you too well for such formality, though I know that you, for your part, are totally unaware of my own small, insignificant existence.

You have probably never seen me. When I came to visit you with my pitiful scribblings, which I presume to call articles, I could get no further than those two dark, awesome, uniformed figures who stand guard at the foot of your stairs day and night.

I, on the other hand, seem to see you wherever I go; in the local shop, on the station platform, at the dentist's even in the privacy of my own little room. Your face, always glossy and perfectly made up, though always somehow different. Your style, always immaculately chic, yet still somehow boldly individual. And your sophistication and knowledge; your talk of the best and latest in the arts and fashion and style, and furniture and cuisine, and all forms of sport and recreation.

You are forever hobnobbing with the famous and talented, whereas I am lucky if anyone comes round at all some weeks; a visit from the postman is a special occasion and I'm sure I'd welcome burglars with open arms and a cup of coffee just to make a break from watching that old black and white TV night after night.

Your pages are always filled with the most healthy and beautiful girls, always so athletic, vital and attractive, so unlike the plain-looking frumps or the ungainly, spotty teenagers you get round our way, who seem to grow prams as extensions of their arms, automatically, at the age of eighteen.

I tried all that 'male grooming' myself for a while, bought all the expensive creams and shower gels from Boots, but I've given up now. I'm resigned to the fact that I'm soon going to be bald AND still have acne, without even a couple of years respite in between. And as for the compulsory Raybans, they made me look more like an ageing Roy Orbison than one of your suave, besuited *Cosmo* men.

Then, of course, there is your continual tantalizing discourse on how best to arrange one's limited valuable time in order to get the most from one's career (or even careers!) whilst, at the same time, enjoying to the full one's 'relationship(s)', while still getting in daily jogging, contemporary dance, squash, hang-gliding and sub-aqua. I'm so career-starved, I'd gladly pay to borrow someone else's, even for a day. I'm 25 years old and I've only worked for one out of those 25 years and that was in a dead-end job, never mind a career!

And as for 'relationships' the only lasting relationships in my life at the moment are with the woman behind the desk at the Social Security and my Bank Manager, and trying to increase the 'intimacy factor' or achieve 'mutual sharing' or 'good communication' with those characters can be difficult, believe you me.

But enough of this pathetic self-pity. I have only to gaze upon you no matter how impoverished and mundane my own life and my spirit is uplifted. You tell me of another world, a glossy, bright world of positive, vivacious, talented people, a world continually turning with new events and new affairs, new directions and developments and releases. An energized, exciting, glamorous world, so unlike the one I see day in, day out. This is why I love you, you are my ideal, my star, my grail. At least when I see you, I see that there can be a better life. It does exist, if only I could enter it.

And so I remain your unrequited but devoted admirer.
Henry Shires

COMPLAINTS AND CORPORATIONS

O Great Computer,

Forgive the presumption of a mere organic entity addressing
you but I felt it was time we got to know each other on a
one-to-one basis. I've been meaning to write for sometime but I
didn't know where to address the envelope, then I realized how
silly I was being – you control the computerized sorting system –
you'll be able to route this letter in the same efficient manner you
direct the rest of my mail (if this means that some inoffensive
calculating machine in Hull is reading this now – I apologize).

I've known of your existence for a long time of course;
whenever I queried anything – a mistake, an anomaly or a plain
old-fashioned balls-up, I was told, 'It's the computer'. Not that
I'm stupid enough to believe there's only one of you – obviously I
realize you have acolytes to carry out your master-plan, i.e. to
reduce humankind to a file of categorized digits.

Before we come to the reason for this letter I must congratulate
you on the clever infiltration. Twenty years ago, for instance,
hardly anyone outside the scientific community was aware of your
existence, now you seem to be the essential pivot of our lives.
Two decades ago we had to take nasty, grubby pound notes to the
electricity shop to pay the bill, nowadays, thanks to a clever
central processor, I can push a few buttons on the building
society's terminal – and pay a complete stranger's gas bill.

I know you're going to claim it's not your fault. You're going to
blame it on the human programmers, aren't you?. Well you may
be right. A French scientist – a scientist mark you – one of your
high priests – remarked that, 'If you put tomfoolery into a
computer nothing comes back but tomfoolery.' However, he also
added, 'But this tomfoolery, having passed through a very
expensive machine, is somewhat ennobled and no one dares

criticize it.' And therein lies the problem. Nowadays if 'the Computer' says your telephone bill is the size of the National Debt – then it is – no matter what common sense dictates. Did you know there is a society for people who've had money disappear from their cash-card accounts? The banks, of course, have absolved themselves of any responsibility. These card-holders are sleep-walking amnesiacs and/or have sticky fingered relatives. Gone are the days when the customer is always right – not if they contradict you they aren't.

You have persuaded us you are essential to the continuance of civilized society. But are you? True, a vast industry has sprung up around you. Thousands labour in the computer industry, to earn enough money to spend on washing machines, videos, microwaves – and all the other necessities that we didn't realize *were* necessities until recently. Naturally all these durables have to be made by you, dear Computer, because you are quicker, more efficient, and hence more cost effective than humans – not *better* though – just compare what humans are prepared to pay for a hand-knitted jumper with what they'll grudgingly disgorge for one from a computer-controlled knitting machine.

The argument you perpetrate is that we need you to produce things more cheaply and hence be more competitive. OK, I'll buy that. Progress has always been with us. I imagine there were a lot of pretty miffed long-bow manufacturers around once the flint-lock was discovered (although I'll bet no gunsmith ever denied responsibility for a backfire by blaming it on a computer).

It's clever to let us think we're still in control. It's not true of course. I mean if we humans *were* in control we'd have directed you to build computerized irrigation systems in the Third World instead of putting some of your acolytes into space-bound lasers that will eventually be able to put down (with unerring accuracy) Mr Bloggs of Acacia Avenue, Peckham Rye, if he should happen to query his computerized telephone bill – wouldn't we?

It's this lack of control that has prompted me to write, dear Computer. Just by filling in a coupon in this country my name has ended up on the computerized address lists of a credit card company in Holland, a stamp firm in Aruba and a magazine group in the USA. I have nothing against these companies writing to me (it makes the postman think I'm important) but what happens if you flip a wrong circuit and I end up listed as a card-carrying member of the Save-the-Lesser-Spotted-Wombat Society? Should I ever wish to visit a country whose Gross National Product relies on turning Lesser Spotted Wombats into handbags I could end up exploring parts of that country's judicial system that I didn't want to know about.

No doubt when today's toddlers, who grip a joystick before they grip a bottle, grow up, we may manage to establish what the politicians refer to as 'a meaningful dialogue' but, in the meantime, there are a mass of people out there with a lot of answers that are looking for a question.

Now I hear your organic cousin in the East is breeding biological computers that can grow, learn and reason things out for themselves. However, until the day comes when we can get a sensible answer from you – as opposed to a logical one – I shall sign off with the thought that is pinned to the wall of our (computer) company office. 'To err is human. To really foul things up requires a computer.'

Yours, 914526078

Dear Tourist,

It is lovely living here. Just at the moment this quiet corner of North Yorkshire is at its most beautiful. The low autumn sun has caught the papery plumes of bracken and tanned them every shade of brown. The tops of the moors are quilted with purple bunches of heather and the hawthorn bushes whose blossom topped the June hedgerows with creamy clouds are now dripping with reddening berries. It is, indeed, lovely here, but you already know that, you are here too.

I like living here. I like to look across that wide moorland view with its mile after mile of fat, scudding cloud and wind-tousled moor. My eyes slowly turn and there you are jarring the view with your no-nonsense red car, blue folding chairs and pink rugs. To be perfectly honest you are not aesthetically pleasing. If planning permission had to be sought before you could plonk yourself so firmly and unceremoniously on the roadside, I, for one, would not grant it. You are an indecent blot on a perfectly harmless landscape.

I notice, Tourist, that from time to time you retreat to your noisy, oil-puffing car to meander down narrow roads looking at The View. I live twenty miles from my work. In winter I skid and slip across the snow and ice and the journey takes thirty minutes. In summer, because of you, the trip takes a quarter of a hour longer. I expect you've heard somewhere that the pace of life is slower in the country. Well let me tell you that it isn't nearly as slow as the fifteen miles per hour that you travel at.

I do try, Tourist, to be charitable, but I don't really understand you at all. Take, for example, your signpost ritual. You drive slowly up to a signpost symbolically spreading its arms at a nondescript crossroads, and you stop the car, slap, bang in the middle of the road. You unfold a large sheet of paper in front of your face, hide behind it, pop out, hide behind it again, pop out and then fold it up. You back the car a few yards, drive forwards a few feet, stop, indicate right and turn left. It is not, I hope, a secret ritual. I know I have been behind you for the last ten minutes, but I don't think you've noticed me yet and I would rather not see the ceremony if it is not meant for my eyes.

Then there are the sheep. Poor tourist, they, for all their woolly minds, have got you baffled. You do realize, don't you, that they live here? They are not planted by the local tourist board to make the unfenced moorland roads look prettier. Anyway here's what to do if you meet them. Just remember that whatever a sheep is doing she will continue to do. If you see an old ewe sitting in the middle of the road you can be sure that she will continue to sit there. She has been nibbling heather shoots all morning and is now indulging in a little quiet post-prandial rumination. The universe is hers to contemplate. Do not drive up to her and hoot with irritation. She will sadly turn her eyes to the heavens in disbelief at your ignorance of etiquette and continue to sit there. Drive round her. If you find a sheep occupied with a gourmet feast of gorse she will continue to be occupied whether or not her woolly hips are planted halfway across the road or not. If a vociferous gossip of a sheep is shouting to her friend across the dale she will continue to do so until all her news is exhausted. So, dear Tourist, the answer is simple, drive round the sheep, you are after all using their roads and they can't see any good reason for moving for you.

I remember, every week, when I lived in the town, that there were half a dozen men in orange vests who came round the streets with a large lorry into which they'd heave the not yet archae-ologically interesting contents of the dustbins. They would have been infinitely saddened if all the bins were empty. I suppose times have changed. Maybe with current financial cuts that system no longer exists. Perhaps I am out of touch, but I must say I don't like the new way. I have been studying it closely. I gather that the general idea is that you, dear Tourist, gather up all your rubbish – the bottles, tins, packets and papers – and drop it item by item at ten-yard intervals as you drive around the country roads. What a sad flotsam from your pre-packed, bio-degradable lives.

Well, Tourist, you will have gathered that I don't much like you. You see everything about you is negative. You look unsightly, you leave litter, you block up roads and you drive into those soft-eyed sheep and their fluffy springtime lambs and leave them dead by the roadside. You cannot even spare a smile as you drive along isolated from the countryside in your car. You show the people and the land equally little consideration. Dear Tourist, I draw to a close now. When New Year comes resolve to change. Come back amongst us next year as visitors who walk down the dale where the wild daffodils grow and enjoy them without wanting to pick them. Stand quietly and watch the acrobatic lapwings tumbling through the air. Do not scare them away with your noise. Smile and get to know the people here. Come to the country with humility and leave behind nothing but enjoyment. And, if you cannot do that, dear Tourist, stay at home. Look at our views in a book of photographs, because, sadly, we don't want you here.

Chris

Dear Bank Manager,

Thank you for your touching letter. It really made my day.
And I daresay you went home feeling excellent about it. Another
self-employed person put in their place. After all you are
God...aren't you?

May I take up a little of your very precious time? I would like to
put a few things straight. I can assure you it won't hurt your brain
too much. Firstly, have you ever looked at my file at your bank? I
presume you do keep all the forms and letters that I have filled in
and written? A word of advice – it is quite useful to refer to this
information on occasion. That way you don't make so many
mistakes. However, if you cannot read I do apologize for
suggesting such a ridiculous thing.

There was no need to bounce my cheque (£8 was hardly going
to break the bank). In my file is a list of cheques received from my
lecturing work. They appear at approximately 4 or 5 week
intervals. They have done so for four years. Now I know this
method of payment does not fit into any of those idiot forms you
hand out at the bank where the day and hour of payment is to be
recorded. However, it might interest you to know that this is
called 'dealing with individuals'. I believe your bank stresses
something to do with its treatment of individuals in its
advertising. I suggest you read it.

Let me explain more simply in the hope that something might
sink into your brain cell – if indeed you have it with you today.
There are some people out here in the real world who work
regularly but are paid erratically. For instance I completed an
illustration for a magazine 5 months ago. I am owed £120. I have
not received the money. One day I will. This is normal practice
for the self-employed. If you had any intellectual capacity
whatsoever (pigs may fly), you would appreciate those who
operate as individuals. A miracle when you think of what we are
up against. Not only do we have a bunch of bimbos running the
country and crushing any form of individuality but we have to
deal personally with our very own fascist bimbos in the form of
bank managers.

I would like to remind you that when you send me letters about
my £5 overdraft it is not your money we are talking about. So you
don't have to be quite so tightfisted about it. Also, if people did

not have overdrafts, sweetheart, you would earn less money as a bank, wouldn't you? So why get your knickers in a twist about £5? Another point – I am £5 in debt. The bank then bounces one of my cheques, knowing that a £500 cheque was to arrive at any moment for my lecturing. The bank then debits my account with another £5 due to 'extra work' in bouncing a cheque. What exactly do you get paid to do in your work? Why is this work considered 'extra'? Did your staff have to stay after 'home-time' to do their 'extra work'? My God you write and talk the biggest load of rubbish ever.

Let's face it, you run an inefficient and unprofessional outfit. Your computers might be brilliant. The staff that operate them are total imbeciles. Last month you lost one of my cheques. When it is found do I get an apology? You forget to pay my mortgage – the excuse is that you are training new staff and it is their fault. But still no apology. I know your office has to share a brain cell but learning to say sorry does not take intelligence. Perhaps one of the computers knows how to say it.

I am sick to death of your crummy letters that I am greeted by each morning. Have you nothing better to do with your time? Perhaps it is the return letters you like? There are pen pal clubs you can join to help this sort of problem. It would certainly save some of your clients from dying of boredom upon receipt of your letters.

Finally I want you to know that you are a very rude, fat and ignorant man. What is more you are so disgusting to look at it is almost pornographic. I feel sure I could prosecute you under the rules of the obscenity laws. Please do not tell me how to live my life and I will refrain from telling you exactly what I feel about your life – if indeed it can be called life. One day I will be reasonably wealthy because I am good at my work. Many other 'poor' clients will also grow wealthy. But you still won't understand. You won't understand that these individuals give you your wage packet. Yes, without us, the great general public (all made up of individuals), you would be nowhere. Kindly remember that banks exist to *serve* the general public. That is the only reason you have a job.

Yours most sincerely,
Carolyn Thompson

Dear Mr Black,

Of course I'll call in to see you next Wednesday to discuss another of my Personal Loan Plans. I can't wait to tell you about the plans for the new bathroom. A few decadent touches here and there of red velvet and gold fringing, gilt mirrors strategically placed to reflect lovingly some old texts of the *Kama-Sutra* and *voilà* – a good clean old-fashioned brothel-look is what I'm after, and it's not going to cost the £2,000 I hope to con you out of either – but I'm going too fast.

Do you remember our first meeting some years ago? It was my eye-bags that brought us together then. Eye-bags run in my family like the Irishman's wooden leg. I had staggered round with them for years, fed up with with nudge nudge, wink wink remarks from colleagues like, 'Good night, last night, was it?' when all I'd done was go to bed with a cup of cocoa.

I had tried everything for those eye-bags – grated raw potato, standing on my head, you mention it, I'd done it. I used to sit at traffic lights making grotesque faces. I'd read a book on the subject of exercises, unfortunately they entailed lots of slow eye-closing. There were many angry car drivers on the A3 in those days. Now, thanks to you and that competent, sexy and wealthy cosmetic surgeon, the roads are fairly safe again. You and he both got your pound of flesh.

That first interview with you was the real turning point in my life. There we sat, me in my All-beige, All-Jaegar respectability, while you questioned me as to what good use I'd put the money to, that's if I got it. Well I was fairly ethical in those days, now I'm a hardened sinner. So to your blunt question – I gave a blunt answer. 'A small cosmetic job,' I murmured, rolling eye-bags in your direction. 'To your kitchen?' you countered. And that's when the downhill slide started.

It was 'The Year of the Kitchen', Knotty Pine, Old Colonial, Farmhouse (French preferably) – burgeoning all over the damn place; in a flash it came to me. *I* was the main fixture in my kitchen – change *me*, and a whole new beautiful dimension would be added to my place of work. That's when I became, if not an outright liar, a distorter of the truth.

Nothing startling happened to my life, I wasn't offered a fabulous new job on TV, Greek shipping magnates didn't beat a path to my door to offer me the use of their yachts and the female stars of Dallas and Dynasty can still rest easily in their beds.

The 'Kitchen Craze' was followed by the 'Extension to Property' era. That was the year I spent a month contemplating my navel and eating bushels of youth-giving apricots, in the High Himalayas. I'm glad I presented you with that basket of apricots anonymously. I really don't want you to go through life faster than me, because we make a great team.

I've become very obsessed with noses at the moment. As a three-year-old I entered into a competition with a mad dog for a meaty bone and he bit my nose. I think I'll leave my nose for a while – it could come under a future heading of 'Operation Double-Glazing'.

So, on Wednesday, when we've dispensed with the preliminary chit chat and you say, 'What new scheme this time?', I'll be truthful, if you could call it that, and say laughingly, with a seductive flash of my de-bagged eyes, 'I'm thinking of taking off On the Golden Road to Samarkand,' and you will smile faintly and play with the forms, and wait, and then I'll come out with my blurb about bathrooms, and costs, and estimates and all sorts of boring details I've picked up from a friend.

Sometimes I have the strangest feeling that you understand me only too well.

Until Wednesday,
Margaret Westcott

154

Dear Antenatal Department,

I know you are all busy and overworked and doing a difficult job. But perhaps you can find time to pause, think, consider – that some mums-to-be may be different and will not easily fit on to your conveyer-belt approach?

I was asked to come in as an 'urgency' to your clinic on 11th September. I arrived with my husband at 10.30 a.m. and was told by your registering clerk that I should tell whoever saw me first in the clinic that a miscarriage was threatening.

This I duly did – and continued to do for the next two and a half hours. But why is it that no one seemed to hear? I was weighed, measured, gave urine, had blood taken, was advised about diet, given masses of booklets, told by a charming dental therapist how to look after my teeth and those of my baby's, filled in endless forms and all the while I kept saying 'excuse me, but I think I'm having a miscarriage,' but no one heard. Meanwhile, my panic-stricken husband was kept waiting in your reception room and shown a video on how to give birth. Two and a half hours later, tired, frightened and exhausted, I re-joined my husband to await my turn to see a consultant. Even though my husband told the sister in charge several times that I was bleeding, the 'waiting list' apparently was sacred. Eventually I lay down gratefully on an examination couch. The consultant glanced at my notes, heard me say I was bleeding, instantly said, 'that's easy . . . you should be in the ward,' phoned up to a ward, and I was suddenly an in-patient in your hospital. Couldn't someone have arranged that at 10.30 a.m.?

But more was to follow. Now, it seemed, I must not walk. A porter must wheel me to the ward and of course the porters were at lunch. So I had to sit on a chair for another 20 minutes before one arrived to wheel me to the ward. Then I was immediately taken for a scan where I was kept for 2 hours and asked to drink a jug of water and then casually told by the woman who did the scan that the foetus has probably died, but let's wait and see. Then anxiety back in the ward was followed the next day by uncertainty and apprehension, while no doctor saw me and I was left all day with my sad and frightening thoughts. I was discharged from hospital on the 13th and asked to return in a week.

Sadly, I did miscarry on the 14th and I must add that I was shown every kindness and attention when I was rushed back to your hospital that night and during the next 3 days of my stay in ward SM9.

But couldn't a harrowing ordeal for me and my husband (this was my first pregnancy and I am 40 years old) have been prevented, if only someone had taken a minute from their 'compartmentalized, programmed approach' to hear me say, 'I'm bleeding, please could I see a doctor?'

Yours in sadness,
Mrs L Woolrych

Dear Chairman of British Rail,

I would like to tell you about a railway journey I made last Wednesday, 28th August, between Birmingham and London Euston after a tiring day's work in the Midlands. The day had started badly as the tube, on which I was travelling to Euston, broke down and I caught the 07.30 intercity service to Birmingham with only minutes to spare. Little did I know that this hitch was an omen of much worse things to follow later in the day.

For my return journey I chose the 17.50, which in fact did not leave until 18.05, but from then on it sped along and before I knew it we were at Watford; my only complaint until that point was about the lack of toasted sandwiches in the buffet car.

Shortly after leaving Watford, however, the train squeaked to a halt again. After a pause the hesitant voice of the guard announced that there had been a power failure and that we might be there 'for some considerable time'. There was an audible sigh as we all shifted uncomfortably in our seats and rummaged around in bags and briefcases for the books, magazines and knitting we had just tidied away, ready for our arrival at Euston.

Only my colleague, Mrs Rosetta Bain, and I thought of moving from the packed second-class compartment to the comparative comfort of the virtually empty first-class accommodation. There Rosetta chewed her way gloomily through a cooking apple as there was hardly any other food available on the train, while I peered out of the window at one or two escaping passengers.

Men in orange vests, who had spotted the escapees, appeared in our carriage and warned us not to leave the train under any circumstances, reassuring us that a diesel engine would shortly arrive to tow us back to Watford, from where another train would take us back to Euston. Pedro, the buffet steward, who by now had little more to offer than lukewarm lemonade and packets of matches, announced his intention of shutting up shop until he discovered how he and the guard, who were both Wolverhampton-based, were to be transported home that night. We very much wanted to know the same thing ourselves.

More than two hours passed until it was pitch black outside and only then did British Rail decide they would after all let us walk down the track to Harrow, where another train was waiting for us. Pedro and a senior British Rail official, who had had the misfortune to be travelling on the train and was now taking charge (and who, by the side of Pedro, bore a marked resemblance to Basil Fawlty), rushed past importantly while we wearily collected together our possessions.

The previously timid guard, whose confidence had now increased to the point where he was calling all the ladies Darling, helped us down a ladder to what we assumed to be the track. In the darkness it was impossible to tell where we were going. We peered at the ground in the moonlight, looking for a safe foothold, as we made our way slowly towards the station, meanwhile rehearsing quotes in case the local press should be waiting to interview us about our 'harrowing' experience. They weren't. Nor was the promised train, whose tail was to be seen disappearing in the direction of Euston as we arrived, breathless, on the platform. A cluster of engineers, who were working there, stared incredulously at this ghostly procession from the train they knew had broken down nearly three hours previously.

As we waited for the next Euston train a group of American tourists took photographs of their bruised feet and the station sign and discussed cashing in the Britrail passes they had purchased only that morning. A queue of passengers, who needed to make urgent telephone calls, snaked around the Station Manager's office. The lucky passenger who had actually reached the front of the queue slammed the receiver down as he heard a train approaching but it sped through the station, tooting impudently.

We were rescued finally at 11 p.m. and we sank thankfully into a corner of the grubby commuter train, only to be jolted wide awake again as a bunch of drunken youths lurched on to the train, crammed on to the seat next to us and started to make passes at the girl sitting opposite. As soon as we dared, we made our escape along the carriage to seek the protection of our American friends.

I finally reached my own front door at midnight, very hungry, flat broke from having paid a large amount of money to a taxi driver and with no leather left on the heels of my shoes.

Tell me Sir Bob, do you think I should go by car the next time?

Yours sincerely,
Helen Wright (Miss)

PS Could you very kindly pass the enclosed claim to your insurance department for their consideration:

Estimated cost of repair to badly damaged leather shoes, the damage having been caused by walking along a railway track in the pitch dark:

On behalf of Miss Helen Wright	£10.00
On behalf of Mrs Rosetta Bain	£10.00

Cost of taxis, necessitated by our unanticipated late arrival at Euston, already scared half to death by our fellow-passengers on the journey between Harrow and Euston:

On behalf of Miss Helen Wright (taxi from Euston to Putney)	£8.00
On behalf of Mrs Rosetta Bain (taxi from Euston to Maida Vale)	£5.00
TOTAL	£33.00

Dear Bob and Sue,

Just a few lines to say thanks. Without your quick-thinking actions on the day we looked round, we may never have bought the house from you.

Thanks, Bob, for greeting us at the back door even though we were at the front. Informal neighbourhood we thought, no one stands on ceremony, everyone uses the back door.

We found out later that there just wasn't a front door key.

Thanks, Sue, for draping yourself over the newly fitted formica work surfaces, well sticky-back plastic actually, as we were whisked through the kitchen. Margot Fontaine(?) (Fontayne?) would have been proud of you poised on one leg like that while the other knee held the cupboard door under the sink in place. I didn't look too hard as I knew you'd recently given birth and I thought you might be raising your pelvic floor or something.

Besides, Bob was drawing our attention to the freshly applied wall tiles, biscuit with sporadic corns on cobs and rafia wine bottles. We chipped them off the day after we moved in.

Thanks, Bob, for pointing out your made-to-measure alcove shelves in the lounge. I might even say they persuaded us to buy the house and were not to suffer the same fate as the kitchen tiles. How are they by the way? Have you made to measure an alcove to fit them in your new house?

We worried about your kneecaps, Bob, as you hovered in doorways while your toddler daughter broke the sound barrier on a tricycle. We now know, the scars in the woodwork tell the tale, you did not usually loiter neath the lintels.

Thanks, Sue, for not opening the airing-cupboard door. I preferred having the cascade of rubber knickers fall on my head in private.

Thanks, for not boring us with the details of how enterprising you both were in DIY matters. Who would have thought that pieces of wood rescued from a bonfire could then be used to make a curtain pelmet? Well not me – that is had I not breathed on it whilst putting up our curtains thus making it fall off.

Thanks for not telling us that the bedroom wallpaper would give us nightmares or that the toilet wallpaper would give us daymares.

I only hope someone does the same for you one day.

Yours thankfully,
Wendy Taggart

Dear Sir,

My family and I have just returned from a Happy Villa holiday and I must write to thank you for its many pleasures.

While foremost in our minds, the following should have special mention.

The accommodations were, to say the least, exceptional, and the approach by rutted country road enchantingly rural. It was an interesting test for our new car springs, and our own fault that we were stuck in the clay for quite a while. We later found enough rocks for traction, and the delay was really immaterial – although we would have preferred to arrive in daylight. Oil lamps are a little tricky to the uninitiated.

Your forethought in providing a security lock was the ultimate in protection, but unfortunately we found access impossible. The local police were helpful, however, once we had located the only telephone box, some five miles away. Subsequently most of the doorknobs came off in our hands, thereby providing Open House! Hunt the screws was fun.

A little covering for the floors would have been appreciated. Chilblains are a drawback on holiday. However, the garden mud does tread in everywhere. Splinters in the floors caused some problems but we learned to be careful of patches where the floorboards had given way.

Pump water, fresh and clear, had – we found – to be primed, and it was some time before we located the nearest stream, across the county border. The novelty of the natural shower must not go unmentioned – a rainwater sprinkle through the ceiling was quite enjoyable, the constant drip did, however, provide a somewhat monotonous accompaniment to insomnia. The mod. cons. too were unusual – and airy! A nocturnal safari through the undergrowth of an untended garden is a privilege afforded to few, and it was our oversight to have brought only one torch, whose batteries ran out. Of course, any lock on the door would have been superfluous expense.

Without electricity we did not, naturally, expect a fridge, but the larder was quite adequate for our needs, and we are all very fond of mice.

The beach and its facilities – featured prominently in your brochure – were, we thought, somewhat overrated. An exhilarating hike across moors and ditches brought us only to the top of the high cliffs. A long, steep slide down was rather hard on holiday clothing, and we were soon cut off by high tide. Unable to climb the steep way back, we were indeed lucky to be spotted by the Coastguard, and the lifeboat rescue was a great adventure we wouldn't have missed for the world.

Your inglenook was a delightful piece of Olde England. Our mistake was in trying to light a fire in it, with wood from the local hedges. Volumes of black smoke took days to clear, and a deluge of black soot from the chimney played havoc with the furnishings. Possibly birds' nests on the roof were the cause of some of the trouble.

We appreciated the little Calor gas cooker, but it was really too small to heat water for the wash. We enjoyed taking our laundry to the aforementioned stream and beating it on the rocks. Unfortunately it would not dry, although hanging for days on your small length of garden string thoughtfully provided for a line. This finally broke, necessitating yet another visit to the stream and a repeat performance. Somewhat hard on modern fabrics, alas.

During the worst summer on record the window wedges were probably intended to keep out draughts, but dislodging one upstairs caused the glass to fall out. We will, of course, reimburse you for this, our error. The bedroom was subsequently beautifully aired, and although the damp sheets posed problems, they undoubtedly calmed our incipient hysteria.

We tried very hard to obey your instructions to 'leave the premises as we found them', but in spite of every effort the rats would not come back.

We would thank you for an unforgettable holiday, unparalleled in our experience, and return your keys herewith.

Might we suggest a little updating of your brochure?

> Yours faithfully,
> Barbara Delgreco (Mrs)

Dear Florist,

My husband is not a demonstrative man – at least not outwardly. As far as he's concerned, giving flowers to a female is something that other men do for other females. We've been married seven years, and it's about that length of time since I received a bouquet of flowers from him. So when he walked into your shop and ordered a bouquet for my birthday it was a rather unprecedented gesture. And when one of your assistants 'forgot' to process the order, it meant more than you'll ever realize.

The date of the order was 28th August. The due date of delivery was 29th August. The date of delivery was – never.

I'm writing you this letter because I've never received an apology in any form – by post, by phone, or, dare I say it, with flowers.

You may be interested to know that on the evening of my birthday I met my husband, along with some friends, for a drink and a meal. He showed great interest in the gifts I'd received, and kept asking if there was anything I'd forgotten. In the end he couldn't restrain himself, and asked if I'd received his flowers. I'm sure he didn't believe me in the beginning when I said I hadn't. After all, people are always sending each other flowers, and they always get delivered – don't they?

He took it well, I must say. He showed me his receipt and a copy of the message I would have received. He even made a joke of it with our friends, telling them the reason he never (usually) sent me flowers was that a budding romance like ours had blossomed all on its own.

The next day he went back to your shop, and was given his money back, together with a cursory apology. As for me, I was left with the rather despondent feeling that it's the thought that counts.

Yours faithfully,
Anne Pincombe

(Mrs A. Pincombe)

Dear Chief Planner,

Re Housing Development – Appleton Hall Gardens

Do you have a dream? I have a dream, that one day the New Town Development Corporation will leave my mother in peace to live out her days without fear of compulsory purchase, or green belt land turning into black belt overnight!

Your dream must have something to do with a larger, shiny new town, spreading onwards and outwards for ever, swallowing up every beauty spot and available piece of agricultural land. Have you ever stopped to think how you could re-develop land which has already been used and is now abandoned?

I am sure you have no idea, as you sit in your slick office, drawing up plan after plan, that your department has dogged my family for 20 years. You knew nothing of the protest march my sister and I undertook when I was ten years old! The banners which we carefully made displaying 'Down with the New Town', were never even seen by you. Even at that age, I was aware of the senselessness of ripping up the countryside for more and more of the same boxes, together with the roads and bridges to service them. However, you did not listen, the Public Enquiry was a joke and the five houses that sat in the middle of fields on a narrow country lane, were blighted and therefore compulsorily purchased by your unfeeling purseholder!

I don't suppose you stopped planning for a minute, to consider that it had taken my parents two years' solid house-hunting to find the place where we could be happy for a long time; a house with fields at the front and back, which was green belt and therefore supposedly sacred from developers' hands. When someone suggested that another bridge was needed to span the already waning ship canal, I think you closed your eyes and dropped your pencil on the map to see where it landed. I suppose that's one way of making a decision, but having done so, fought all opposition, bought up the land you wanted, why did it take 20 years for NOTHING to happen? The house still stands, you in fact sold it back to parents of friends of mine, for HALF its market value.

Meanwhile, my mother and father found what they thought was another small haven of green belt. My father was there six months and died. My mother still lives there, ten years on, having recently re-married and you have followed her.

You bought land adjacent to hers, from an old man who needed the money and sold out, at a healthy profit I have no doubt, to one of those pretty, upmarket box builders, who have now started systematically to rip my mother's haven apart.

I ask you, what should my mother do now? Should she take up her roots and move again, only to have her peace shattered and land taken away once more, or should she stay put, shut up and accept the inevitability of once more being on a housing estate through no fault of her own, but because of your shortsightedness?

I also wonder what all these property developers think of having constantly to drop their prices, when they find that they too have been conned and cannot find enough people to fill the boxes they have built – albeit £80 – 100,000 boxes.

The last thing I would like to ask you is do you sleep comfortably at night in your own house (which is surrounded by green belt – yes, you managed to safeguard your own property and future)? Are your dreams hounded by bulldozers and diggers, ripping up your garden and smashing your house down? Did you ever really care and did you ever really have a dream?

Our family have lived a nightmare!

Yours faithfully,
Helen Hughes

Dear Dustman,

Tom Crabtee is always telling girls to do their own thing and speak up for themselves but how many black slavegirls has he met?

Of course in some areas we're very much in demand. We're very quiet and discreet. Cecil Parkinson has two in London and four in the country and Prince Michael keeps six just for old newspapers. Mind you, Val is always telling him never to throw anything away. You never know how valuable an old bit of paper can be.

I'm digressing again. That's the trouble with being stuffed with a load of old rubbish all the time. How can a girl improve herself on fast food and *Private Eye?*

I was just getting into *Ayn Rand* when madam tossed in a melon and reduced it to a pulp. I could have cried. I got my own back though. I asked Big Bee in to finish off the jam tart and when madam came to throw in her SDP membership card Bee buzzed right into her face. Madam screamed and sprinted into the house quicker than Zola Budd.

There I go again. I should have persevered with that 'Teach yourself Concentration' article but I kept dropping off. What I wanted to say was I do wish you could take a bit more care with me. You're such a big strong chap and when you whisk me up in your arms and lead me up the garden path I really quiver. I drop things here, there and everywhere and madam gets very uptight about that. Then there's the water. Every time it rains I get soaked to the bin and I feel like flipping my lid – if you ever put it back on. You usually fling it on the back lawn and I can hear madam going on about 'paying all those rates just to send the councillors to Moscow'.

I'd better close now. I can hear the master staggering out with a few bottles and you know what he's like when he's loaded!

Yours every Wednesday,
Plastic Dustbin

(Brenda Bercow)

This is a letter that I sent a couple of months ago to a well-known book club that persisted in sending me books that I hadn't ordered. Incidentally, it did the trick; no more books!

Dear Sirs,

> I've written to you nicely
> But things are getting worse
> Perhaps you'll get the message
> If I put it into verse.
>
> Your books keep on arriving
> And though I often spurn them
> You don't seem to believe me
> And I have to return them.
>
> So please tell your computer –
> (Computers – how I hate 'em)
> This is your final warning
> This is my ultimatum.
>
> I'm rapidly approaching
> The limit of my tether –
> I don't want any more books –
> Not this month, next month, *EVER*.
>
> But if books keep arriving
> I won't complain unduly
> I'm quite prepared to keep them –
> But as a gift –

> Yours truly,
> B. Baker
>
> (Betty Baker)

Dear Croydon Corporation,

POOPER SCOOPERS FOR CROYDON

On a recent visit to New York I was strolling along behind a little old lady with a Yorkshire Terrier. The dainty scrag-bag (the dog that is!) was all kitted out in a petite pink silk coat to keep him warm and a matching pink ribbon to keep the hair out of his eyes. As he suddenly stopped to do his necessary daily business, the old lady neatly and deftly took out her shopping bag and removed what appeared to be a miniature dustpan and brush and proceeded to sweep her little treasure's titbits into a brown paper bag. A bit further on she neatly disposed of the paper bag into a side-street waste-paper bin. *Finis!*

After my initial reaction of dissolving into fits of giggles on the sidewalk, what suddenly and forcibly impressed me was the fact that this action was not only exceedingly considerate to other pedestrians but was at such little cost to the dog owner. On relating this story to some American friends, I was to discover that this is law in the State of New York, and the owners of dogs must dispose of their animals' souvenirs in this manner! This has resulted in a great boom of 'pooper scoopers' which are widely available to be purchased in all the local stores and supermarkets in every possible shade and style. They have become the dog owner's most necessary fashion accessory; the prerequisite co-ordinates of any dog owner would be incomplete without a pooper scooper to match dog-collar and lead!

On returning home I read that the local council in Barking (ha! ha!) had voted to pass a similar by-law on a temporary basis as an experiment. In consequence, surely the quality of life in Barking has greatly improved for the local residents who no longer have to walk along the pavements practising their best dodgem-racing-car tricks; not to mention how much happier the local cats and dogs must be – after all their noses are closer to the ground! The trees and shrubs, much relieved to be rescued from this overkill of life's natural fertilizer, must have actually found space to branch out and grow.

Altogether this is without doubt a move in the right direction and one which any forward-thinking council should be encouraged to follow. Knowing how Croydon Council succeeds in being considered as such I would ask you to initiate Croydon into the joy and power of the pooper scooper. Despite signs stuck on lamp-posts warning that people will be fined if found fouling the footway (or should I say their dogs found fouling the footway!) unfortunately lots of people do not take a blind bit of notice and carry on whistling regardless, while their dogs use that same lamp-post to aim their best shot at with the precision and accuracy of a sniper. Don't they do well!

I know a dog's gotta do what a dog's gotta do, but please, a little decorum is in order – one can't expect a dog to tie a loo roll to its tail and potty train. It's really up to the proud owners to take care of that side of their dog's affairs, and up to us lesser mortals to summon up our best pompous glare if they are caught slacking. The trouble is I can't quite see us Brits going off merrily making citizens' arrests of people not using pooper scoopers, but equally find it hard to believe that New Yorkers are actually using them. Surprisingly they are. It is in fact rather amusing to observe a six-foot body-building Rastafarian from Harlem out walking his boxer dog carrying a Ghetto Blaster in his left hand, and a pooper scooper and paper bag in his right!

Apart from anything else, Croydon must without doubt boast the most healthy dogs in London. Perhaps local dogfood manufacturers put Ex-Lax in their Boneo but, whatever the reason, during the heat of the summer months (you remember summer, it comes between spring and autumn) the heady aroma from some footpaths, could put the stink bomb out of business. No one likes it, hopscotchers are the best at avoiding it, bicyclists slalom either side of it, and for the blind it is just a case of getting out your white stick and hoping for the best.

I suppose there is the advantage that it does keep you alert in the morning, sleepyheads stand no chance. Walking to the station becomes a major feat in getting from A to B intact as you pick your way through a minefield of treacherous pavement. I have yet to meet someone who has never got 'caught' – sooner or later your number is up and you don't get through the obstacle course, whether you gingerly choose each step or hold your breath and brazenly dash through with abandon. Your booby prize is an embarrassing journey to London Bridge not quite knowing where to put your foot, let alone your face, as people first of all contemptuously sniff the air and grimace, and then open the window before they systematically attempt to track down the culprit by staring out each person in the carriage until signs of guilt are detected by a blushing face hiding behind a week-old newspaper.

So come along Croydon Council and get the ball rolling. Let's get this show on the road (or should I say off the road) and follow Barking in being innovative leaders of the United Kingdom in clearing our pathways. We've had the Year of the Child, so why not let 1986 be the Year of the Pooper Scooper. They say Cleanliness is next to Godliness – Get Pooper Scoopers for Croydon and make it a better place to live!

Yours faithfully,
Suzy Adams

Dear Mr X,

Just who do you think you are kidding? Last Christmas, on my way to the bright lights of the West End, I was sitting in my car when I heard a screech of brakes. Was it a bird, was it a plane? No, it was your client losing control of his vehicle and ramming it up my exhaust pipe.

Needless to say we all jumped out, took a quick look at the damage, exchanged details, and wished each other a happy Xmas before driving off into the festive moonlight.

Obviously the Christmas spirit has since dissipated. The collision was certainly not a simple bumper to bumper as your client slewed into my car at an angle. His was, I recall, a brand new car. Mine WAS a Renault which would have folded up had a flying crisp bag hit it.

The impact resulted in the nearside rear panel buckling and the exhaust nigh on giving up the ghost. Whether your engineers found red, orange or sky-blue pink paint on the rear has about as much relevance to this issue as whether a fish needs a bicycle or not. There must be a new clause in the process of insuring cars these days. You seem to be saying that your client can ram his lovely silver grey car into mine and get away with it. Even the slightest collision leaves some mark on one or another of the cars involved yet your client's car – somehow – had 'absolutely no damage or marks'. Have you been in touch with the *Guinness Book of Records*? I'm sure you deserve a mention.

The fact of this matter is that your client skidded into my car and drove off after a perfunctory look at the damage. I was motionless at the time. Your client is to blame. The time has come to pay up.

By repudiating my claim are you saying this incident never occurred? Surely not. I can only assume it means it was I who was asleep at the time of the accident, instead of your client.

You can, of course, repudiate until you are blue in the face. For a company who never makes a drama out of a crisis, though, you are certainly making a mountain out of a molehill on this one.

I would be very much obliged if you would stop playing silly games and get on with the claim. It is now nine months since the accident and you should have had enough time to give birth to a solution – or do I have to do it by Caesarean section?

Yours in anticipation,
K. Austin

Dear Miss K Witherington,

I am an offended customer.

I am the lady you sent to the 'Day Dresses for the Mature Woman' section of your benighted store on Tuesday of last week.

Oh I'm sure you remember. Let me jog your memory.

It was just after opening time and you were sorting out the blouses whilst carrying on a conversation with your colleague on the other side of the 'Just In' department (incidentally, I hope you and Rick have sorted out your little problem...?)

My three-year-old son was with me – is it all coming back? I am tall and dark haired, but I freely admit to the gentle sheen of grey making its presence felt. Oh the agony of the decision – to colour or not to colour?

Anyway, there was a perceptible pause as you registered the fact that a middle-aged mum had wandered into your 'sanctum' – by mistake surely – (forty is middle-aged isn't it?) then the merest raised eyebrow as you went on to discuss the various attributes of Trev in China and Glass. After about forty-five seconds, however, I knew I was being watched. I am not normally one to be unnerved by the scorn of the young, but when your offer of help turned out to be the suggestion that I go and look in 'Day Dresses for the M.W.' I was so speechless with outrage that I left.

Now, you may be committed to the belief that anyone over the age of twenty-one qualifies as the 'mature woman', but it is not your business to offend customers by pigeon-holing them according to how many years they have clocked up. Whatever my age is, it does not give you, your superiors, buyers or designers the right to dictate how I should dress, cut my hair or in any way conduct my life.

Your reaction is symptomatic of an all-pervading attitude that those women in their 'middle years' should also be middle-of-the-road. Well I am here to protest. In my head and my heart I am somewhere between fifteen and twenty-five, and I have every intention of remaining so, and if I choose to take my children to school in Lurex boots and a see-thro' jumpsuit, that is my affair.

I would also point out that I am in possession of an adequately functioning intellect. I am condemned on two counts you see, anno domini and domesticity. The existence of offspring clearly indicates to many that the mother has rigor mortis of the brain.

Don't be misled; I have triumphed in the struggle to elevate my mind above the level of the washing line. I refuse to be forced into circles where the conversation is exclusively concerned with potty training, the price of kids' socks and where best to shop for my freezer. I can still read. I still hold opinions on subjects other than the comparative merits of knitting wool, and I can still choose how I *dress*!

If, in the autumn of my life, I am frivolous, spontaneous, obtrusive, my children will either be embarrassed beyond bearing, or regard me as a lovable eccentric. You will probably be learning what it is to be tolerant of the young.

Yours sincerely,
Janet Dawn

PS I subsequently bought a *very* unsuitable dress from the shop over the road!

Dear Sir,

Although much correspondence has passed between us over the years, I have never written of my true feelings towards you. We always took refuge behind the formalities which preserve distance and anonymity. The time has come to set the record straight.

Do you remember the first letter you ever sent me?

> I note that your account is considerably overdrawn. Our papers show no arrangement for this facility. Would you kindly introduce funds to restore the balance at your earliest convenience.

Rather than respond as requested, I flushed the missive down the nearest convenience, along with the red telephone and gas bills, and the 'let's just be friends' letter which arrived in the same post.

The plumber who came to unblock the drains was the only nice thing that happened that day. He made me tea and shared his philosophy of life with me; there was no pile of shit so big that it couldn't be shifted with patience, knowhow and a good plunge.

I was so low I used to be jealous of the bathwater. Why can't it be like that for me, I thought – a whirl and a gurgle, and that would be it. So, you'll understand, I really needed the new stereo to cheer myself up, and the puppy to keep me company. I must admit that the vet's bill for surgical extraction of a box of Brillo pads was a totally unexpected setback.

I crushed your next two letters unread into the dog's bowl, to stretch the Winalot. Times were hard. I realized the crunch had really come when you sent the one marked 'urgent'. You certainly know how to hit where it hurts. That reference to 'agents for the collection of debt' was vicious, it gave me nightmares for a week. Me and Bilbo huddled in a cold dank cell in the debtors' prison, deciding which was going to eat the other. So I arranged to meet you.

I set out armed with my full battery of aggressive wit. You epitomized all that was depraved and despicable. I was adrift in a hostile world – no job, no partner, no home to cling to. There you were in your oak-panelled office, caring for nothing but my paltry overdraft.

You destroyed me that day. You were so sympathetic, so bloody nice. You left me with nothing to hate, but myself.

A couple of meetings later, I would have sworn you were 100% human – though I was taken aback at the suggestion that we discuss my finances over dinner. I'll never forget your expression when I took out my cheque book and offered to pay.

When you first detailed your proposals re future management of my account, I was reluctant to agree. I was loathe to render complete control of my life to my bank manager. Then I thought, well, why not then, Hell, this is absolutely wonderful!

You know the rest of it. From sheer desperation to love everlasting via a massive overdraft. I don't know if I can ever tell you how happy I am, but I want to try. All of me, from scalp to toes, is bursting with love, although admittedly, about halfway down, lust enters in. I'm longing to see you again; to watch you shed those efficient official clothes and step into the bath, and to see you emerge vulnerable, desirable, and mine.

I must conclude this statement now. Our daughter has pulled the door off the washing machine, and she and Bilbo are having a lovely paddle in the soapsuds.

See you tonight –
Your doting, spendthrift,
Wife, XX

PS Darling, could you see your way to securing us a little loan? I've got this yen for mountain air and blue skies – Switzerland maybe? Just you and me, and lots of credit . . .

(Jacqueline Hotchin)

Dear Mr M,

Why do you ignore my messages?

Why won't you respond?

I have tried to catch your eye so many times, and this is my last attempt. Be warned! Drastic steps will follow if you maintain this stony silence.

I'm writing (sorry, typing) this during a quiet spell in the office, and if I sit at my VDU pounding the keys it fools everyone into thinking I am madly and enthusiastically busy. If I were to put pen to paper rather than key to paper, however, *they* would all know that I am enjoying a quiet spell and pounce.

Please don't think that I am using you to fill in a bored half hour; I would write to you even if I had to miss my lunch to do so. Indeed, since we last met those few weeks ago, I have been meaning to send you a letter to let you know how much I have been missing you.

It may come as a surprise to you, but I am not alone in this as my husband has, if anything, missed you more than I. And you didn't even think he noticed, did you? Since we have been without your visits, his mornings have been lacking in something which, though I curse and cajole, I have found no replacement for. He glowers with disdain at the bleak, black coffee on his breakfast tray and eagerly sets out for the office where he knows his needs will be met. What can I do?

I regret now that last note I left for you in my haste. If only I had made myself a little clearer, I feel all would now be restored to contentment and comforting routine. Ah well, what's done is done.

Since I last saw you we have had a lovely holiday. We 'did' Europe by car (I'm sure you noticed its absence from our pathway as you crept past our house each morning), with tent stowed in the boot, phrase books to hand and travellers' cheques safe. We even got as far as the South of France would you believe. We returned looking fit and glowing with health and sunburn.

I only wish our paths had crossed since our return as I am sure you, of all people, would have appreciated the brownness of my visage and the sun-kissed look of my tresses, instead of the usual pallor and dullness with which I greet you every morning.

If you really must know, I missed you even when we were away

– though heaven forbid hubby should ever discover this damning confession. I feel I have betrayed him, though I really did try to get used to living without you.

I took to the bohemian lifestyle pretty well, I felt, and really enjoyed the French bread and brie with which we broke our fast each hot and drowsy morning. But some things just cannot be replaced. And what you have to offer is one.

It causes much distress in our household that you choose to ignore these missives. I cannot think why you do, but perhaps it is true what they say about out of sight being out of mind. (Though I personally have always preferred the one about absence making the heart grow fonder.)

But can't you see, we're back in view now.

It isn't in my nature to beg. Oh all right then, I beg you, dear Mr Milkman, leave us a pint this morning just like you used to.

I promise we won't go away and cancel you again. Well, at least not for another year.

Yours milklessly,
She of No. 14

(Christine Magee)

Dear Mr Crawford,

I am writing to protest the amount of the bill you sent me today. It really is far in excess of my expectations and I am not too impressed with the work either.

First and foremost, I asked you to create a driveway at the bottom end of my garden. *My* garden mind! I am still apologizing to my next door neighbour, Mrs Coot, for the demolition of her garden wall. I know that you rebuilt the wall but did you not notice the bed of roses next to it? I'm sure you must have felt it. (Mrs Coot certainly did.)

Secondly, I asked you to build the garage in such a way that it would blend in with the rest of the house (and not lower the tone of the avenue). Since when did pink pebbledash blend in with red sandstone? I really think you ought to do something about it – and I don't mean painting it either (one of your workmen's suggestion).

Thirdly, where is my weeping willow tree? I arrived back from work last Friday (20th Sept.) and it was gone. I told you that I didn't mind if the driveway was a little bent (and I don't know why your workmen found that phrase so funny) so long as the willow tree was kept intact. So, where is it? And no, I don't want a rhododendron bush in its place. I want my tree!

Fourthly, about your workmen. If I'd wanted a carpet patterned with muddy footprints leading up to the toilet I would have bought one! I was perfectly within my rights to tell them to do it elsewhere. How was I to know that one of your workmen would fall into the stream? He shouldn't have been doing it there anyway. (Haven't you heard of Man's Pollution?) And no, I don't think I was being heartless in not letting him into the house to change. What would the neighbours have thought?

So you see, I really feel I should get a substantial reduction from this bill after all that I have been through.

Yours sincerely,
L. J. Miller

PS In answer to your question – I would love to go out to dinner next Saturday – I presume you will be paying?

(Lisa Jane Miller)

Dear Father O'Brian,

You probably have little recollection of who I am, from the full house that turned out in their Godfearing Sunday-best to seek absolution. I feel compelled to write, however, to let you know how impossible it is to live by the rules of the Catholic faith, which you recited from your pulpit throughout all of my youth and most of my married life.

As a young girl I attended mass, duty bound by my sanctimonious parents to rid myself of all evil thoughts in the Lord's house. I remember little of what was said in those days, save for the pangs of hunger before communion.

Years later as a wife and mother I still went to mass, partly out of conditioned fear and safeguard against retribution, and partly to seek refuge from the chaos of family life. I recall quite clearly, the day I began really to listen to what you were saying. That morning, breakfast had ended in a tense silence as was often the case, with the children wide-eyed and nervous over their cereal. I had hurried to church with a desperate, sick feeling in my stomach, grateful for the keen air and relief of outdoors.

The church smelt of burning candles, incense and the odd whiff of heavy perfume and stale tobacco. I suddenly felt very claustrophobic, and to stave off my discomfort I concentrated on your sermon. As I recollect it was ironically based on the act of adultery.

I use the word ironical as the parish had an abundance of women which placed a heavy responsibility on the male populace, to which they responded with an equanimity and selflessness which in most cases would have been admirable. Adultery was not so much a broken rule at home, but a means of reinforcing the community, and a task to which my husband took with great alacrity.

After leaving church that day, I resolved honestly to evaluate my faith in the scriptures and to put them to the ultimate in practical tests – in other words to live by them. I was twenty-five years old then, and expecting my fourth child in as many years. The joys of expecting had long since deserted me, and I still remember that empty feeling when the pregnancy was confirmed. I had never contemplated using contraception, as it had been drummed into me from my teens that the female role was that of wife and mother. After all, what greater skill but that of procreation.

I knew two women my age, who after three children each had plucked up sufficient courage to go to a clinic for a course of pills. Mind you, they were so afraid they took it in turns to go, and shared a tablet every day. Needless to say, the method proved less than satisfactory and they were both pregnant by Christmas.

Abortion was another forbidden solution in the Province, the only way out being to lose the baby. In retrospect, there was a high incidence of miscarriage in the neighbourhood. My mother always asserted it was something the government was putting in the water.

I digress, however, from the fact that early into my fourth pregnancy I decided to put God's laws to the test and see if they actually worked, if they applied to our times. In the depths of my loneliness I started to look around me and inside me. On the outside I beheld nothing by violence, poverty and dereliction. I kept asking, why, if God was all powerful, could he allow all this magnificent creation to go to waste? Perhaps it had only taken him seven days to make, but we, like rats in a capsule, were forced to take part in the test run. I use the word forced advisedly, as God in his infinite wisdom had closed our only loophole and made it a cardinal sin to take life – even our own.

I saw no compassion or love, or even charity as I looked around that Christian community, which evidently was not hearing you either, Father. It suddenly struck me how easy it was to have faith in the Catholic church, as effectively you were handing over responsibility for your thoughts and actions to the priest. A confession a week made the prospect of hell very bleak!

When I looked inside, I found nothing but a big black hole, with no feelings left for my husband and family life. We were children creating more children out of ignorance and misplaced trust. I could not turn to my parents, who were too busy leading a respectable life to let my problems intrude, unless they were likely to cause public humiliation.

That night I made my first decision and prayed to a different God from yours, Father. This one listened instead of condemning me, and the ultimate decree was for my own good.

I moved away from the neighbourhood over a year ago, and now live with my three children, the youngest of whom is just starting school. I work now and take full responsibility for myself and family. I no longer go to church, but I pray every day to the God that gave me the confidence to start again.

I hope you are not offended by this letter, Father, but I wanted to let you know how different life is from our side of the pulpit, when the person preaching is not a loveless wife, pregnant for the fourth time. I am not sending my address as this is not a confession, Father.

May your God keep you,
Mary Finch

(Jenny Armstrong)

YOUR BRILLIANT CAREER

Dear J,

I expect by now you're wondering why I didn't show up for
work on Monday. No, it wasn't my time of the month. This is
more like the time of my life. You see, I'm not coming back to the
office. Your talent for delegation will be taking a short breather
and for a while you'll be taking all the credit for your own work,
instead of mine.

I've split. In more ways than one. The half of my personality
that was hooked on winning approval, paying my way, showing
I'm better than any man, has finally broken away from the other
me, the one who's finally realized that there's more to life than
testing myself to destruction.

I know. You don't drop out at my age. Dropping out is strictly
for kids, and for forty-five-plussers, bingeing on redundancy
money or pursuing lost youth. Whereas I'm in my prime. I run
your company single-handed and the only recognition I seemed to
have earned is financial. Yes, you paid good money for me, I
agree, and it is indeed a damned nuisance when an expensive
piece of hardware ceases to function . . . You silly man. Didn't
you realize I'd have worked for much less, quite happily, if you'd
treated me as an equal?

Well, I'm up to here with being Superwoman. I'm fed up with
pandering to your double standards. When I'm assertive, I'm
considered aggressive, when you're aggressive, you're considered
forceful. When I complain, I'm called paranoid, when you
complain, you're called assertive. When I'm anxious, I'm labelled
neurotic, when you're neurotic, that's being a perfectionist.
When I'm late, I'm late, when you're late, you've been
unavoidably held up. And when I'm sick, I'm playing up,
although when you've got a hangover that counts as being sick.

When you don't get home for dinner, you don't expect your wife to gripe, because you've bought her off with a nice house and a Harrods account card. When I don't get home for dinner I make do with beans on toast.

And yet, ironically, I've put up with all this precisely *because* you don't care, you don't interfere, you give me a free hand because you know I'll do it right. Have you any idea how hard it is for a woman to achieve that kind of freedom? It took me so long to get my wings that I've lived in fear of being grounded. I was offered another, similar job. I didn't tell you about it. When it came to it I chickened out, I opted for the devil I knew. You. So I'm not putting all my dissatisfaction on to you. I accept my full share of the blame. That comes easily, to us women.

I've been salting a bit away. My FY money, I call it, I'm sure you can work that one out. Here in Hungary, you can still buy a basic shack and a plot of land for under £1000. Eastern Europe isn't all grey. This has got to be the most fertile place on earth – drop a used match and next year there's a sapling. Coming here has taught me that you don't need consumer goods to have a high quality of life – for life, like the soil, gives back what you put into it. Up to now, I've spent my life mowing and weeding, rather than sowing and planting. I want to turn the neat, tidy garden of my life with its paved patio and window boxes, into a field with an infinite capacity for growth.

I'm going to give it a year, until my money, or visa, runs out. I don't want to come back until the yeast's finished working and there's nothing left to prove. No more half-baked living for me.

She's gone mad, you're thinking. She had it all. Perhaps she's pregnant and doesn't want anyone to know. Perhaps I am, in a way.

My last service to you will be to write the ad for my replacement.

DYNAMIC MD SEEKS PA. UNIQUE OPPORTUNITY FOR AMBITIOUS SECRETARY TO SUPERVISE DAY-TO-DAY RUNNING OF FAST-GROWING COMPANY. LONG HOURS BUT UNIQUE REWARDS. HIGH SALARY, COMPANY CAR, MUST BE ABLE TO TRAVEL AT ZERO NOTICE. SO IF YOUR SOUL IS FOR SALE ...

Mine was. But now it's free.

Yours no longer,
L

Dear Sir,

There are a few things I want to say to you before I leave and I shall start with the carpet. The office carpet is brown. Actually its a deeply boring brown combining the charm of dried cow-pats with the gingery flecks of a cigarette tip. The manufacturers call it 'cognac'. The carpet also smells of old tea-leaves by the 'cashmere'-coloured radiator. Perhaps you have never noticed. Perhaps you are blind. I'll tell you some more. There is an ocean of shoe-sole impressions, puckering streaks of dragged furniture, new stains rising from old stains, cheap human tracks where beige people leave debris in your light-tan heaven. The fibrous droppings, off-white crumbs of colour that descend from files, pockets, ash-trays, bodies, handkerchiefs . . . you know the sort of thing. The litter of dead nerves rendezvous in my mind conspiring to stop thought; still the breath of ideas and life. Perfect office decor: an assortment of non-colours searching for their ghost-like souls. They can only hint at some former glory lost amongst our almost-fawn filing cabinets, pale-mustard filing cupboards, teak doors and teak tables, recasting their dusty shadows endlessly – trying to get it right. What colour is a shadow? Well in here its 'soiled history', a nice shade of vending machine coffee. Very popular. Yes, beverage stains in triplicate fester on dead carpet; ex-carpet, a carpet which has ceased to be. What's happened to colour? Where do these aborted pigments and dying pastels come from? What 20th-century alchemist conjured: pampas, magnolia stipple, smooth-grey, nearly-black, sonata (dirty peach) and forest (pond slime)?

In front of me I can see the fire extinguisher. It is raging red today – burning with geraniums, wild skies . . . a shepherd's delight of poppies, ice-cream pinks and red-hot blushes. It's the red of school paint and crayons, bursting with questions, dreams and passions. A red you have never seen in all your beige life. Iridescent. Distinguished. Improbable. The red of sabotage and survival.

Yours faithfully,
Jane Cooper

Dear Prospective Employer,

No, I am not pregnant, nor do I plan to become so in the foreseeable future. No, I'm not married, engaged or living with anyone, and if Cupid does fix me up with a congenial Romeo from Plymouth or any other foreign part you may rest assured that I shall not desert you to go gallivanting around the countryside after him. I want to live here so if you employ me you've got me till death, retirement or winning the Pools us do part.

Well, that's answered all those essential questions that employers usually ask at interviews, now perhaps I can tell you something about myself. No, I know I haven't filled in an application form nor sent a CV, but I've been writing those repeatedly over the last three years and they haven't got me anything more than a pen-shaped groove on my index finger and a rising concern over the cost of stamps. Tell me, do you actually read them at all? I seem to have been slogging my way through life, or rather through university existence, under the delusion that qualifications actually qualified you to do something. Very funny I'm sure. I realize now that the string of letters after my name means nothing more than total confusion to everyone who reads it. It's obvious really – if employers *wanted* someone with qualifications they'd probably make application forms with enough space for you to list all these dubious achievements without having to resort to writing like this to fit them all in...

Anyway, that's why I'm writing a letter instead. I thought I could tell you about ME – the real me, not the number on the examination paper nor that impassive intellectual chain of letters that alternately weighs me down then trips me up and makes me degree-sick in the process. I mean, I was an ordinary person once and I'm sure I could be one again if that's what you want. How can I be over-qualified? I don't have to be clever all the time you know, I can be just as stupid as the next person, even more so if I don't put my mind to it. In fact I have quite a gift for it...

Cut. As you were. Where was I? Yes – ME. What am I really like? I'm hard-working (that is, I think I'm hard-working but I won't really know unless you give me some work to do, will I?), moody, sarcastic, unsociable, pessimistic, reasonably unbalanced (emotionally and physically), in possession of an archaically obscure sense of humour, never bored and ... oh yes, I'm honest too. What more could you want? I'm unique. Just think, I'm offering you the chance to become the first person to employ one of me. Haven't you ever wanted to be different? After all, good business is based on the ability to take risks and if you can't do that then I ought to be in your job anyway.

What can I offer your business? – Blood, sweat, toil and tears. For a generous remuneration I offer toil. For a modest remuneration you'll get toil and tears. Sweat? – well that's just something else I've got a talent for, and I promise blood as a free gift to any member of staff who starts making lecherous advances. Unless of course he's young, handsome, single, rich ... but I digress. What else? Well, I'll even agree to coffee-making as long as you have it de-caffeinated with skimmed milk and no sugar. I flatly refuse to turn you into a fat, toothless addict just because you've no willpower. I don't want to be blamed for all your problems, I've enough of my own, and if I'm going to have an ulcer I shall have one of my own and not be palmed off with a hand-me-down from you.

So why do I want the job? Do you really have to ask? This is the truthful application, remember? There's a limit to how politely I can answer this without mentioning the dreaded word. I could say, as I usually do, that I'm looking for self-fulfilment, intellectual stimulation and an opportunity to further my career, but why should I have to lie? It all comes down to wherewithal in the end, to liquidity, to resources, to financial provision, to money, money, MONEY! Oh, I feel better now I've admitted it. In fact I feel positively virtuous now I don't have to co-habit with my guilty secret any longer. It's not as if I want stacks of the stuff but it's hard to feel self-fulfilled when you can't pay the mortgage, the washing machine leaks and a car with air-conditioning means one with holes in the floor that squirts muddy water up your legs whenever you drive through a puddle. As for intellectual stimulation I'm getting plenty of that trying to figure out how to provide nutritionally balanced meals on a ration of 1,000 calories a day and six pounds thirty-nine a week, whilst philosophically pondering on how to expand my career when I haven't actually got one to stagnate let alone expand.

So there you are. I hope by now that you're as convinced as I am that I'm the right person for the job. If I'm not perhaps you'd be good enough to create another job especially for me. Ignore me at your peril because I think I'm getting the hang of this application lark and I don't intend to give up now – so why not offer me a job and get it over with quickly? Or I may just turn up on your doorstep ...

Yours expectantly,
Carol M. Chambers

Dear Mr Lane,

I am Valerie Thurley, the lady who came to your office for an interview on Friday 30th August. After twelve years devoted 'service' to marriage and children I wanted to rekindle my elusive self-confidence and return to being employed for monetary gain. No one knows the total humiliation I felt when you interrogated – I mean interviewed – me.

You sat looking at me as if I had emerged from a time warp – OK I haven't got this year's latest fashion frills. Any clothes I've bought the last few years had to fit in with my budget and lifestyle, so it's not surprising that they look like Oxfam rejects.

You sensed straight away that I had the confidence of a drowning duck and revelled in the macho 'I Tarzan you Jane' or 'I Rambo you Rif-Raf'. My only hope of a place in your company hung on my past academic achievements – 8 'O' levels, 2 'A' levels. You shot those down, didn't you? Not an academic mention except 'No degree Mrs Thurley' and 'You don't seem to have any secretarial skills'. That was just whetting your appetite – an hors-d'oeuvre for the kill. 'Do you feel you are able to adapt and fit in with all the new technology?' Yep – like a Triffid you lashed me with that one – I felt like old mother hen – I'm only 35! 'Do you feel you will be able to communicate and get along with everyone?' 'Well I was an air stewardess before I got married,' I feebly uttered in defence – feeling my only worth must lie in what I was and not the decrepit apology for a person I am now. 'Yes,' you said and muttered quietly (but not inaudibly), 'that was some time ago.'

The crescendo to your arrogance was however the moment when I was 'pleading my defence' – i.e. qualifying my validity in applying for the sacred post – you actually picked up the telephone and began speaking to your secretary, without the merest regard to me! I should have walked out of your office. I was eminently suitable for the job – it was only part-time receptionist/clerk for goodness sake!

I have no idea who you employed and thought right for the job but in retrospect I know that because I wanted the job so much I would have worked brilliantly for you. I would have smiled ceaselessly at your clients and acted totally conscientiously.

Well, I am having a much needed holiday at the moment – to

'restructure' myself. I'm glad I bothered to write to you, it has made me feel 'cleansed' somehow and maybe it just might make you realize that candidates for employment have got feelings! I already feel I am worth more than you could have offered.

Mrs Valerie Thurley

Dear Caroline,

You can hardly have failed to notice my stifled yawns at Sophia's dinner party last night. I was so enjoying the evening until you came out with the wearisome and predictable comments about my job. 'I don't know how you can do it! . . . it must be vile . . . and every day. Thank goodness there is someone who is willing to do such a job . . .' Your exclamations still ring in my ears. You have probably completely forgotten the surprise and ill-concealed disgust which you displayed on learning the nature of my profession. Do fire-eaters, snake-handlers and toilet attendants have to put up with comments like these? I'm only a dentist after all.

Do pathologists find themselves being told how revolting their job is? Do guests sigh sympathetically over the dinner table imagining their loathsome daily task examining blood and urine samples, and worse? Are gynaecologists plagued by questions about looking into unmentionable orifices all day? Are sewage workers patronized by those who pontificate on the good they do for society?

These questions ran through my mind while deciding how or whether to reply to you. It crossed my mind to answer what I was thinking: 'But, Caroline, I feel so sorry for you! How excruciatingly boring it must be to be an accountant! Spending all day looking at lists of figures – how appallingly dull.' I thought it, but I didn't say it. Why, then, in our respectable middle-class circles, is it considered socially acceptable to tell me how disgusting my job is? I have good and bad days at work, but on the whole my job is as fascinating and stimulating as it was on the first day, seven years ago. It looks as though it will continue that way, too.

'How can you tolerate looking into people's mouths all day?' What do you think I am looking at? You use your mouth for life's most pleasurable activities yet you think it is a sewer. You kiss, eat, make conversation, smile and, just as you wash your face in the morning before you go out, you clean your teeth. Thus, our regular patients have respectable mouths and not sickening chasms with obscene recesses full of last week's breakfast. Patients who consistently turn up for dental treatment with dirty mouths are told so in no uncertain terms. Complex treatment is never carried out unless the patient can keep his mouth clean. So we spend most of our day dealing with a relatively wholesome environment.

We have our share of worries, but these concern the time spent *not* looking into people's mouths. Staffing problems, bureaucracy and practice expenses; these are far more likely to give us a harassed look.·

So next time you are introduced to a dentist, please purse those shiny red lips and spare us the offensive remarks. We've heard it all a thousand times before.

Yours wearily,
Catherine Phillips

Dear Mum,

I DID IT! I HAVE WON THE JOB OF MY DREAMS!

I have just finished the day's photo session and it went like a dream. The first day all the other models were given their assignments for the week, but I was taken out to lunch and, completely out of the blue, offered the 1986 Pirelli Calender assignment, which will be taken as soon as is practical upon arrival back in Britain.

Mum, I just can't believe my luck! Considering the hardships of the past six years and the battles I fought to get to the top, now finally having made it the feeling is indescribable. So many times I tried and failed, yet thanks to you and the rest of the family spurring me on ... well what can I say? So much is owed to the family's faith in me.

It wasn't so long ago people made fun of me at work, and made all those hateful comments; if only they knew how much inner hurt was caused.

Do you remember those days when I used to come home from work crying my heart out because of all those nasty, slanderous comments. Now though, in the light of my success, I can no longer feel hate towards them, only sorrow – after all they are stuck with a nine-to-five job and your new daughter has made it to the top. Mum I'm so happy, so very, very happy.

To think back to 1979 when I was very ill and had to see Dr Randell at Charing Cross Hospital, who diagnosed me as needing a treatment programme to effect a complete hormone change; and now, after all the surgical alterations and the final surgery back in May, and taking all the crap people both on the street and at work threw at me, finally *your* Steph did it!

I'm not the only sex-change model on the market and there is no way I can compete with Tula; but at least Tula and I are good friends and let's hope it stays that way. Be a great shame to lose a friend like Tula. She has also been a great insentive to me and a great inspiration. Please forgive my spelling mistakes but I'm so terribly excited with everything.

There's a few weeks' holiday coming up soon and the question is, how would my favourite person like a two-week vacation in *Rome?* Please say you will come, you'll love it.

Jill (the model who shares my hotel room) says she has heard through the grapevine that I'm in line for a part in the new James Bond film. Me ... A Bond girl ...??? Can it really be happening???

Still, you were right, it doesn't pay to try too hard. The laid-back attitude really does work.

My engineering job will probably go down the tubes in the light of these 'other' offers but I could make enough money to retire on working as a model.

We have another week and a half to do out here in Barbados then we are all off home to Rainy Britain.

Mum, I'll see you soon and hopefully grab the chance to come back down to earth again and a good cup of English tea.

Give my love to all.

Lots of love,
Steph

PS You know what they say 'if the mosquitos don't bite the bed bugs might'!

(Stephanie Robinson)

Dear Headmistress,

I thought I would drop you a line just to let you know how a 'social butterfly' (your departing words to me) has got on in this world nine years after I said goodbye to you and the school.

Having been forced into the painful decision that I would never make it as a scientist, thanks to failing my science 'A' Levels – I must admit I tend to put this down to the pathetic facilities our school provided and your commitment to the male orientated society that 'girls should only study arts' – I decided to join the 'butterfly world' of independent television and try my luck here as a budding socialite. After seven wonderful and best-time-of-my-life years, I am pleased to say (and I revel in what this must be doing to your ulcer), I have been recognized as an independent, serious and dedicated individual who has finally achieved the goal of Programme Director.

I have loved every minute of my 'ladder-climbing', which adds to the pleasure of my work, and in some ways have to be grateful to you for not only blocking and diverting my career path, but also for the basic training you and the school instilled in me during the seven years I spent there – what invaluable experience it was to have spent numerous hours washing and stacking hundreds of smelly, plastic beakers; sending the junior girls to their dormitories at night; ensuring they say their fourth set of prayers for that day; turning out the lights and finally patrolling the corridors to make sure that no one spoke after 'lights out'.

Finally, I would like to thank you on behalf of my parents (whom you managed to squeeze thousands of hard-earned pounds out of) and myself – whatever else you did or didn't do for us at that school, here's one person who came out a fighter and a survivor against all odds.

Yours sincerely,
Jane Hambly

WHEN YOU'VE GOT FRIENDS

Dear Jane,

This is very probably the last letter you will receive as Miss Simpson. Tomorrow afternoon will transform you into Mrs Graham (some feminist you are!) and although you will always be Jane to me, things will never be quite the same again. Even after all the months of frantic preparation and the last few days of absolute chaos, I can hardly believe that the great day is about to dawn.

When you read this letter in your bedroom of our little house, I will be busy at the hotel overseeing the final preparations for your reception. I am glad now that I won't be with you to help you dress despite my annoyance earlier in the week when I learned that your mother and sister wanted to keep this honour to themselves. I want you to read these words, understand my feelings and then never mention it to me or anyone else again. Will you do that for me? Keep it even quiet from Tim. One last secret for us to share.

I said I wanted you to understand my feelings but this may not be easy as I've only just begun to understand them myself. When we first set up home together five years ago, it was never meant to be permanent – just a quiet spell in our lives to recover from our respective traumas before taking up the reins of life again. And we did, didn't we? We recovered and made our home into a warm haven where everyone felt welcome and comfortable. Remember the sad tales we have listened to, the children we have looked after, the celebrations of birthdays, promotions and Christmases and all the nights we sat up for hours just talking, completely careless of the early morning start? And how our friends envied us! Anna and Jane, so well suited. So happy together. Despite our dissimilar backgrounds and tastes we complemented each other so well. We stopped looking on our situation as makeshift and instead made it into a very happy way of life.

Suddenly Tim appeared on the scene. I remember well after your first date with him how you came home, woke my up and we giggled till dawn drinking coffee and smoking endless cigarettes. After this the dates become more frequent and gradually, very gradually it stopped being you and me with Tim in the background and became you and Tim with me floating on the edge of your life. You stopped telling me his little foibles and became secretive and preoccupied. You stopped smoking because Tim didn't like it. You started to lose interest in the plans we had made for summer holidays and Christmas. We drifted along, you on cloud nine, me smouldering with discontent which burst into flames of fury and envy when you told me you and Tim were engaged and were to marry in three months. I was so angry! But you were my friend, I loved you. I should be over the moon that you were so happy. So I determined to join in, make the most of it, share your happiness and excitement. But as you know, as you *must* know, Jane, it didn't quite work out like that. From all sides, your family, our friends, even my family, encroached, full of plans and presents and joy for you. I felt forgotten and left out. Every time the phone rang it would be for you – your mother with questions about your frock (would it clash with the icing on the cake!), or caterers or photographers or Tim, always Tim. Neighbours stopped me in the street to ask about you, saying how happy they were for you, isn't it wonderful? No one ever once thought of the effect your wedding would have on me except to say, we will have to find a man for you now, ha ha ha. So I withdrew into a shell of resentment and self-pity, never wanting to hear another word about Jane's wedding. We couldn't even talk to each other any more – you were so busy, I was so sulky. And then, since last week when the pace became frantic, I realized these were our last few days together. I tried really hard. I'm pretty certain you noticed that, didn't you? You were so relieved that I was taking more interest and I felt so ashamed that I had made you unhappy. When you asked if we could spend the last evening of your single life together having dinner, I was so thrilled. Suddenly I felt good, no more confusion or bitterness, just at ease and happy. I'm even beginning to get excited about tomorrow.

So tonight I will be on top form, I'll make you laugh like I used to and we will drink good wine to celebrate the occasion. I won't get sentimental about our separation and maybe you will be a little miffed at my nonchalance, but hopefully this letter will explain all. I just couldn't face you with these words in case my voice betrayed me.

And so Jane, dearest Jane, I wish you well. I know you will be happy, I've known it all along. I'll visit you in your new home, I'll be Godmother to your first child – you owe me that! – and if our relationship has to change, then I accept that.

Today I rejoice for you, my dearest friend.

Anna

(Ann Abell)

My Dear A,

Well! you've done it now! How brave you are! It was lovely to see you again... and marvellously you are just the same – funny, cuddly, a wine-drinking, chain-smoking phenomenon on little 'Ernie Wise' type legs!! – not totally wasted talents for someone in 'Light Entertainment' m'dear! I returned from your wedding reception totally overcome, and not only because of the alcoholic intake, but rather because of all the emotions and feelings of nostalgia that the occasion had stirred in my breast (both 32″ cups!), particularly after all our reminiscings of times past. It's wonderful and rare but with true friends it doesn't matter that you've been apart for years because when you do meet again all the past shared experiences are so vividly remembered and re-created and you return to that instant rapport. I know you think of me as intense, highly-strung and neurotic – and that's when I've had a good day! – but on my return home I was so restless that, in a positive paroxysm of activity, I completed two lots of washing, hoovered the entire downstairs, dusted what little furniture I possess, and even annihilated a couple of cobwebs, only then collapsing in an untidy heap, luckily rescuing the goblet of Amontillado, to think of you and our days of flat-sharing of, incredibly, as long ago as the 1960s!

Isn't it a shame that men rarely seem to have close friends or, more sadly even, ever seem able to have someone with whom they can share their deepest feelings? I have been especially lucky in feeling sufficiently secure in our friendship always to be able to talk to you completely freely and intimately without feeling afterwards that I'd made a complete fool of myself!! Thinking of, and seeing, you again made me feel that it was important – without embarrassing you too much – to write telling you how much I value your friendship. Even I, who can talk about most things – and my enemies would say I do, and at great length – would find it impossible to make such a confession face-to-face. Sophisticated as we humans are it's a sad fact that we find it so difficult to tell someone how much they mean to us. A deep regret of mine, and sadly their deaths now make this omission irrevocable, is that I never actually ever told either of my parents that I loved them very much. I tried to show my feelings towards them of course, but wouldn't it have been wonderful if I could actually have committed myself verbally as well? Why are we *so* afraid of admitting how vulnerable and dependent we are on other people, and why is it only in desperate moments of crisis that our reserve is broken down and we finally can accept that we cannot survive without such support?

When you telephoned to say that you and Jeremy were getting married – typical of course that I was 'out' and had to recieve this momentous news second-hand! – I suddenly and quite selfishly was concerned that our friendship would become less important to you. Why can't our thoughts and actions be pure and unsullied by possessiveness, jealousy or other negative emotions? However, before this twenty-year-plus friendship comes to an abrupt halt on your part, I admit that almost immediately my better instincts conquered; my selfishness was replaced by genuine feelings of happiness for you both; and a real hope released that you will have a really happy life together. After meeting Jeremy I realize that he is a very 'special' person too – your sojourn as a bachelor-girl has finally been worthwhile m'dear, and I'm convinced that in the years to come you'll be the envy of the Richmond Senior Citizen Social Set as the 'Darby & Joan Supreme' – both a living contradiction to Thomas Hardy's dire pronouncement that 'All romance ends in marriage'!

Alas! my life is now so different from those carefree days with you in Camden Town – although amusingly your dear mother always referred to it as 'Regents Park' and endearingly still does, bless her! – closeted as I am in an almost exclusively domestic environment sans career, sans social life, but definitely avec responsibility! I know that the halcyon days were sometimes slightly clouded by the odd 'tiff' when you would terrifyingly stretch your torso to its full and incredible height of 5ft 2ins and immediately exit to engage on dastardly deeds with the duster, myself retreating to my own quarters to write a letter home. Most fortunately these upsets were rare and, if you remember, my darling Dad always responded to any of my missives with a train ticket to Ramsgate by return of post: a sufficiently strong enough reason on my part for reparation of any rift between us! Despite all the traumas of our respective love-lives, I think the most vivid memory of those days is the humour we shared – I've seldom had occasion for a good 'chortle' since – and the fact that despite our very different personalities, not unexpected from a typical stubborn little Aries and a schizophrenic Gemini, we miraculously just 'got on'! They were good times! I shall always be grateful to, and have fond memories of, The City Literary Institute and in particular J.P.'s Drama Class where we first me. I remember particularly your actually impressing the lovely, but definitely effete, J.P. with your superb evocation of 'FIRE' – on reflection I'm still amazed as to what you found possible to do with your long black hair!! I've got to thank you for a lot of happy memories.

I suppose I must now end this letter as I am in danger of becoming maudlingly sentimental... and I don't want poor Jeremy to return from his honeymoon – of all holidays – to renew your Kleenex supply, as *you* are rather a 'softie' too... but don't change in any way.

Love and 'God Bless' to you both,
F

(Hilary Howard)

Dear Baggins,

Here I am sitting on a train that is taking me away from London, and away from the possibility of seeing you again.

Yesterday I approached the Chinese Restaurant with a strange sense of dread. What folly to arrange to meet you there. I was happy to find the place relatively empty. It felt OK to sit there. It was just like any other Thursday afternoon. The place is more a café than a restaurant. I like watching the waitresses as they fold paper napkins and tease each other in an Oriental manner.

I decided to wait in case you had been delayed. I asked for tea only, and after a long conversation in Chinese with the boss the waitress brought me tea in a chrome pot with a plain white handle-less cup. I sat facing the door and experienced endless shivers of fear as the shadows of unknown people passed by.

You did not appear and I found myself wondering if you would ever wait for me. What a curse imagination is. How we trap ourselves into games of folly. I decided to cheat and left sooner than I had planned. Only when I was walking away did I begin to feel safe.

Why did I ask you to meet me there? I had certainly dreamed of a scintillating conversation between us. I had imagined all our elegant repartee. You would be keen, but not too pressing, and I would be able to yield, but not too quickly – it would have been the perfect start to a light-hearted affair.

Of course you may have guessed this and decided to avoid me. There was a certain *frisson* in not knowing if you would be there, but then I realized sadly and calmly, that I have spent my life chasing such notions. I have sat in cafés and bars waiting for romantic events to happen to me... maybe it is because I met my 'ex' by chance in a Soho bar. Previously he had painted my portrait and won a prize, but I had resisted his crazy amorous advances – so why was it that, four years later, I fell into his arms and married him far too speedily? It was the end of the swinging sixties. I stayed at home with the babies whilst he noisily destroyed himself and our marriage in every hippy joint in town. Eventually my survival mechanism clicked into place. I went home to the country with two children and a sense of futility. We were divorced quite painlessly. One afternoon, ten years later, I bumped into him again when I was on a day trip to London. I failed to see the similarity of events then or later... we talked quite sensibly, he said he had moved back to London and ever since then I have longed to meet him again. I would go and sit in pubs hoping he would turn up. I told myself it didn't really matter – so sure was I that we would meet again.

Eventually I realized I was dancing in the dark with images of the past. Life is like an Escher drawing.

How does all this affect you? Well, you were there with me in the Kismet Club when I faced this final thrust of melancholia. No one noticed that I was agitated. We were with a crowd of friends and I was outwardly as cheerful as usual, only you seemed particularly kind to me. Later we all went to the Chinese Restaurant. Then the strangest thing happened to me: I fell in love with you. It was like the proverbial thunderbolt – one minute we were laughing like friends and suddenly I felt this powerful sensation of love. Thinking about it later I remembered all the nice things you had said to me over the years, and how you had admired me. I had laughed and pursued that hopeless affair with a mutual friend.

Somehow I had the idea, this summer, that you too had come to the same conclusion: we could love each other. I envisaged a communal warmth, lying in bed talking to each other, moments of passion, even a trip to foreign places – you would be an excellent travelling companion – extrovert and generous!

So this is why I sent you those gently provocative postcards, and arranged an open-ended rendezvous. When you did not appear I told myself I was pleased not to have to face reality – good or bad. Next day I jumped on a bus and there you were – at least it looked like your back, your shoulders, your black leather jacket. The seat was empty beside you but I did not dare sit there. I passed by and sat nearer the front... The conductor came and I bought my fare. Perhaps you heard my voice? – I became aware of movement, and you, if it was you, hurried off the bus just before my stop.

I turned round but you had already gone downstairs. The bus paused and I saw your shape turning the corner, going down a side street – if it was you I wondered where on earth you were going. I tried to reason with myself that you would not have run away. If I'd caught your eye we would have laughed and chatted as before.

But still there is a question mark hanging over me like the sword of Damocles. Could it be that you were equally afraid? Just tell me quietly and firmly have I got the whole thing wrong or do you love me? Did you too feel that force between us as love crashed out of the apocalyptic blue?

As it says in that old Bob Dylan song: When we meet again introduced as friends don't let on that it was once your world...

Yours in love and friendship,
Augusta

(Augusta Crowe)

Dearest Audrey,

I know you haven't heard from me for months and as usual I'm looking for you to soothe my bruised ego! I reckon you've got it made Audrey. Stuck up in Norfolk with your bloody farm animals and health food. Walking your kids to school every day through fields and getting involved with the PTA whilst I'm a dreadfully lonely lady trying to make a career in the television industry. You're the only one I can turn to – you're the only friend I've got that's not trying to claw up other women to get on – or so attached to my other friends that you would not be able to resist telling them. I don't want anyone to know that I'm going through a weak phase emotionally at the moment. Oh don't worry – I'm still with Laurie... but only in body. Our jobs are driving us apart. He's always away on location and I'm stuck in the cutting rooms. Do you know, when I got out of secretarial work and into assistant editing, I thought at last, a male orientated job (the pay is *so* much better!), but all I've done is make tea and carry really heavy film cans almost collapsing under the weight but smiling and refusing help 'cos I want to be equal. It's a joke. Although I love my job, it's made me terribly maternal. I work mainly on wildlife programmes and most of the films seem to be about the creature's sex life and treatment of the young. The last programme I worked on was about the mongoose and had the babies, who can't see very well, hanging on to their dad's dick sucking like mad thinking it was a nipple! Where does one look? The look of excitement on the daddy mongoose was quite disgusting!

Of course, it's the last thing Laurie wants. A family I mean. We are so up to our eyeballs in debt with the mortgage that I could never give up work. He dropped a bomb on me the other day. I had just got over his fling with a production buyer (I've since found out that she'd have a frog if she could stop it hopping) and was enjoying an expensive lunch out with him when he said, 'I really do think we should be more independent, I mean, I don't suppose we'll go on much longer. We're bound to have a row and then – well, we'll have to make out by ourselves and I'm afraid that you've so few friends here that you won't be able to cope.' I couldn't believe my diamond-studded ears! He could have waited

till I'd finished eating. So there we go, another illusion shattered.
I'm feeling all right about it now. I didn't eat anything from the
moment he told me (I always lose loads of weight when he upsets
me!). I suppose I wasn't planning to eat again until he told me
that he didn't really mean it and that I really am the best thing
besides a film can. I'm sort of marching around with a new found
enthusiasm for everything, realizing that it's little old me who has
to pick up the bits whilst he picks up the bits with tits. I'm
making a useless feminist. I don't trust other women and I long to
have babies and get married!

I even drove to Cambridge last weekend to see if I could pick
up any graduates. I mean, at least they're brought up properly
and what mother would class as 'decent men'. I will never get
involved with a man in television again. The only ones with
sincerity are wearing wedding rings. I always thought that men
who wore rings were terribly insecure but now realize that they're
just trying to keep their trousers on!

Do you know, one terribly drunk film editor said to me the
other night in the bar 'the trouble with the contraceptive pill is
that it's taken all the fun out of sex. We used to be so scared of
getting a woman pregnant that we'd put hairbrushes, Brut
bottles, etc. inside her and it was a turn on. Now there's no
excuse to do that any more.' What a weird thing to say. I hardly
know him! The men who don't wear wedding rings never
mention their wives – or are really rude to them on the phone.
The other day one such male answered the phone and said, 'Look
I'm really busy at the moment. Can't it wait? Yes I know it's
Amy's third birthday tomorrow. Yes I'll pick up the ice-cream on
the way home,' and slammed the phone down with a sideways
glance at me as if to say you women are so trivial. You should all
be on your back in the kitchen.

Of course I'm still in love with Laurie. And what is worse, he
hasn't told me to go...only that I will go eventually which is like
being told you have some dreadful disease that will one day kill
you...but not yet.

I know I have to get out while I still hold my head up and
desperately want you to ask me to come and stay – I was thinking
for about six months. Does that sound crazy? I want to go into the
country and get out of television for a while. Hopefully I'll meet a
rich farmer who'll lend me his landrover and make me happy. Do

you think I'm asking for the moon, Audrey? Please write back.
You're always so sensible and full of good suggestions. I've always
admired you ever since you ran off with Father.

love,
Mary

(Mary Whitby-Jones)

Dearest and most mischievous Jude,

How can I possibly accept that you're not willing to play with me? *Of course* I'm playing games – so are you. So what? What we need to check, in my opinion, is only whether we're playing by the same rules – there are so many different sets of rules – don't you find it all a bit confusing too sometimes? So please think about yours. Here are some questions and observations of mine so far: please consider them before you laugh them off.

What made you think the stoned romantic poem I wrote on the back of the postcard I left in your house was about you?? As I recall, the picture on the other side of the card was breathtakingly beautiful – to me anyway. There were about seven small black and brown girls with flying pigtails, tight curls, expressive faces, each one uniquely beautiful. They danced along in a line, some tugging the slower ones impatiently by the hand and laughing together at each other's antics. Totally natural, alive with fun; teasing each other with the best of childish innocence in their eyes. *That's* the quality I love best in my women friends – including you (and the rest of us) the night I wrote the card. So yes, it was inspired by you, but not by you alone.

A long time ago in Berlin I read a book by a lesbian (Vera Stephan?) called *Shedding (Enthäutungen?)*. I was amazed and delighted to find another woman whose weird thoughts were no weirder than mine and who dared to shout them from the rooftops. She sounded a lot happier than I was – not difficult at that time of my life. I was involved then in an obsessively stuck, semi-lesbian, romantic, cruel, kind, smothering, terrifyingly *secret* relationship with a wonderful woman who was as scared as I was but not as committed. She still phones me occasionally – usually when I have visitors and am unable to tell her as clearly as I'd like to how much she still means to me. I cling on to the memory of the innocent laughter we shared most of all. And cry when I remember (too vividly) the shame, the pain, the confusion – and the occasional bursts of pride, which gradually diminished in our last year together. She is precious to me still for these qualities: pride in innocent fun; simple laughter; easy, close familiarity and comfort. We confront ourselves in each other when we can rise to honesty: sometimes it hurts like hell until you can see the funny side. Now she's married to a boring farmer. Her

211

voice (that low and sultry, familiar Israeli tone) warms me to the
bone and she hears my delighted response – in English, because I
can't be as quick-witted in Yiddish as I need to be with her. Our
conversation has always been lyrical – skipping through subtle
tones and shades of meaning; warmth and withdrawal; a dance. I
fear she may have abandoned me now to give her full attention to
her new marriage. Wonder if she'll be back some day? Recently
she's been in my thoughts a lot and sometimes I miss her.

Mostly though, I'm keeping myself too busy to think too much
– ever since Jess left town four months ago. We were very close
for four years and since she left we've both been through a lot of
difficult changes far too silently, stoically and independently –
until I finally cracked and exploded in an angry letter which hurt
her. That was not my intention. But it shows me we need time
together to talk and cuddle and eat and drink and pass the time of
day with each other. Seems like light years and no time at all since
she left.

I've busied myself with a whirlwind of social activity – quite a
shock to the system of a hermit like me. This has involved me in a
number of quick-change acts: daughter, friend, lesbian, friend of
friend, sister. Then back home to my role of everyone's reliable
confidante through trauma and crisis. There's a lot of it about.
And me? – I'm still steadfastly (sometimes hopelessly) looking for
a playmate, someone who can summon up the energy to have a
good laugh and a dance and a rap. I have begun to find the odd
one here and there amongst my women and lesbian friends. At
times I love and *need* the ghetto mentality: the solidarity, I
suppose, and sharing secrets in the certainty that I will not be
received with damning judgements – indeed that I will often be
rewarded with incredulous empathy. What a relief to feel *equally*
foolish and strong, knowing we will gladly lend each other
whatever strength we can muster when necessary. The feeling of
connection is very powerful for me at times like that – it's like
wish-fulfilment and I do tend to get a little carried away at such
moments.

So it's hardly surprising that I fell in love with you at first sight
(oops! 'false patriarchal consciousness': error no. 1) and simply
and purely because your eyes promised fun and laughter and
innocent, light-hearted games. Open games, girls' games, with no
one in sight or earshot to spoil them for us by misunderstanding,

labelling, spitting, trying to make something suspect or shameful out of our precious happy moments which we have worked so hard to be able to create for ourselves.

Jess once said: 'I refuse to let *anyone* rob me of my innocence.' I'll second that.

With mischievous thoughts from Molly Malone
(that impossible romantic you met on your travels)

Hello Folks,

Greetings! . . . as you know, this is the first letter I have been permitted to write since qualifying for membership of the Institute of Chartered GAs. Those of us who have successfully completed our training and have overcome the most arduous and rigorous tests and survived the probationary period, are permitted, as a reward, to write home to their nearest and dearest.

I know you must all have had a bit of a smile at me, for striking out on my own with little or no experience, but knowing you were all behind me, gave me help and support throughout the past period of indoctrination. You might like to know something about our training programme.

As you know we GAs cover a vast field and in order to function proficiently we have to collect data and absorb a great deal of knowledge (for instant recall), but as we are not allowed to gain knowledge from first-hand experience, our observatory senses have to be keenly attuned.

At first, being a rooky, I was given all the odd-ball and off-beat jobs, one of which was a watching brief on a human lifespan. It was at this point that I discovered the overriding obsession humans have with something which we know is limitless but to them is their most precious possession – TIME. They have terms such as light years, centuries, down to seconds and – hold your (as they say) breath – hundredths of seconds. Now I ask you – what is a 1/100 of a second in *real* time?

Anyway, back to my training course. I had been assigned to look after a female human. I was lucky, because I think the females are more interesting than their opposite numbers, because they seem to be responsible more for the care and survival of the race than the others who appear to spend a lot of effort and energy killing each other, at first with clubs and stones and later knives and through all manner of things like lances, arrows, gunpowder and, their latest discoveries, atoms and lasers. While all of these gadgets can be most helpful for the advancement of humans, in too many instances they are put to work for the wrong reasons. But I must not digress. To resume: I had to see that my little charge arrived all right and did not strangle herself on her umbilical cord, then make certain she received the requisite number of thumps in the right place, to

214

ensure oxygenation. For a while I was kept pretty busy fending off viruses and ensuring that as few germs as possible bothered her, that the pram did not run away, etc., etc., little ordinary things like that. Then followed a jolly carefree period with no inhibitions and little or no formal discipline and minimal restrictions, apart from benevolent supervision from elders; my little charge had little to bother her and spent her waking time enjoying herself. I, in my turn, had little to occupy me as my opposite numbers were doing an excellent job on her parents.

As with everything on Earth, conditions change, and Joan, as she was now known, had some of her freedom curtailed by having to attend school. A period known as the happiest days of one's life by those who are far enough removed from them to remember only the good times.

I found as she got older I had more to do, as potential hazards seemed to increase in direct proportion to her mental and physical development. I was kept pretty busy as she had added swimming, cycling and horseriding to her everyday activities which included going to and from school on a fast-moving primitive transport called a bus and often hurtling through holes underground in a tube. Getting to/from and on/off these things was even more hazardous, having to dodge faster-moving objects propelled and driven by individuals quite oblivious to the basic laws of force, speed and safety.

It would take too long to elaborate, but suffice it to say that our little heroine managed to survive the odd fall, bump and bruise, and I feel I deserved my preliminary certificate attained at the time of her exit from childhood into the adult world. Quite an achievement for both of us.

At that period, the place where she lived was having a boisterous and lively disagreement with some other community, and violent activity was taking place, particularly from high overhead, where individuals in flying machines hurtled down lethal contraptions that caused a great deal of damage and loss of life. As you can imagine, I had my work cut out and was kept on alert 'round the clock', as they say.

There were seldom any idle moments but it was most exhilarating and offered me numerous opportunities to practise my craft. When hostilities ceased other problems, like her future, had to be looked at, and, after a few narrow misses and one or two little jolts, I managed to steer her on to a fairly smooth and not-too-twisted path.

My job with her is now complete and most of the hard work is done, and so I have been relieved of my command which has been taken over by another branch of the service which specializes in the more tranquil period of life while still maintaining vital vigilance.

While writing this I see my name has come up on the assignment board, and I must sign off now as my expertise will be required soon by another, as yet unborn, human, in a modern hospital in a place called Mexico. I have a feeling there will be plenty of work for many of us to do there.

Love to all,
E

PS Write to me soon c/o The Institute of Chartered Guardian Angels at the usual address.

PPS I am writing to you from the luxury of Joan's motor caravan in which she and her husband are touring America. They are keeping a diary as they follow the early settlers' trails from east to west of that vast land north of my future border.

(E. McPheely)

Dear Diana,

I've had a hectic time since you've been gone. Let me fill you in on a few events.

Nick and I were invited to a hunt ball the other day and the theme was India during the Empire and I went along to Enyd's to have my hair scraped into an appropriate style for the period. I had to wear a tiara and this was firmly anchored into position and heavily lacquered. I crept out of the hairdresser's with the hood up on my coat, only to come home and find Nick showing two customers around our garden. There's not a lot one can say to two complete strangers when wearing a tiara, ringlets and wellington boots. Nick introduced us and then promptly left me to make them coffee as he had to sort out a problem in the garden centre. We made polite conversation and then they left. I don't know what my appearance has done for the customer relations department. I haven't seen them since.

After that I had to go shopping in Safeways to get some food. Nick refused to come with me, so I had to phone Lynn and Mo to give me some moral support. You can imagine the uproar. I buried myself headfirst into freezers and Lynn and Mo followed at a discreet five paces behind me, dropping 'Your Ladyship' whenever the store manager was within hearing distance. By this time my dress had become more bizarre. Not only did I still have my tiara on and wellington boots, I also had my barbour jacket and sported a Safeway shopping trolley. Several people in the car park looked aghast at this spectacle and the car-park attendant curtsied as I went past (he should have bobbed his head only!!).

The evening was a hoot. One of the women on our table called Debbie rushed up to me halfway through the evening asking, 'You'd dance with a stranger, wouldn't you?' I thought the question rhetorical and answered, 'Yes I'll dance with anyone, I'm not proud.' To this she replied, 'Oh good, yours is the one with the white jacket.' So I danced with this stranger for a while until his girlfriend/wife dragged him off the dance floor, much to the amusement of my party who were all watching this farce from afar. The evening ended without much more ado.

I went back to the Colposcopy Clinic to get the all clear last week; it's an amazing place. The League of Friends pay for all this marvellous modern equipment, which should belong to the star-wars programme, and the consultant gynaecologist (who's a wonderful man) has to put up with an Ever Ready torch as the Health Service won't buy him an anglepoise lamp!! As soon as they put my legs into the stirrups and raised me up, I collapsed into a fit of giggles; although I couldn't see what he was doing, I could imagine him peering into the darkness groping around with his torch.

Please write to let me know how life is treating you.

Lots of love,
Lynda

(Lynda Smith)

Hi Di!

Well! If I hadn't seen it, I wouldn't have believed it! How on earth did you manage to miss the *aeroplane* to Austria, for goodness sake? Mum shouted up the stairs that there was a postcard from you and, expecting snowy alps, what did I see? – the Tower of London. No one but you could have done it. The last call for the flight is not for the baggage – it's for the passengers! Anyway I hope you enjoyed your stay in London – the rest (or change) will do you good.

Life here carries on much the same as usual. I bought my first house last week – or rather it's all going through at the moment. I've been frantically looking through all the papers for interesting second-hand furniture. So far I've found an antique pine bed and a beautiful three-piece cottage suite. My one problem is storage. They were too good bargains to miss so Dad's promised to clear out the spare garage for me and let me store it all in there. The house (cottage) has beams (something I've always wanted) and there's an open light-oak staircase leading up to the first floor. I've got three bedrooms so there's plenty of room for you to come and stay should you wish to. Peter's promised to buy me a fridge for my joint Christmas and birthday present which is sweet of him. Talking about birthdays, it was his thirtieth last week. I still can't believe it. Maybe he'll start to grow up now. But then men never really seem to, do they?! I bought him a copy of *The Times* from the day he was born – he was delighted. I can't remember if I told you but he's on this health food fad at the moment so his birthday tea was made up of cauliflower cheese with broccoli. I quite enjoyed it actually, except that candles don't look quite right on cauliflower!

I was modelling the Marilyn Martin of London bridal outfits up in Edinburgh for three days last week. It's such hard work. I can sit in my office all day typing, on the phone, etc., but standing for hours on a set is so exhausting!

We stayed at the Dahusi Castle Hotel, a real castle with the restaurant in the dungeons. Quite frankly the castle was all we saw whilst we were there. All the work was done between 8.30a.m. and 7p.m. and then we were all too exhausted to do anything. Richard, the director, kept trying to persuade us to go out in the evening, but you can't have late nights doing that sort of work. The brochures should be out by October, and thereafter in various bridal magazines. I'm so sick of wearing wedding dresses I may well just wear a black nightie should I ever have the presence of mind to get married! No doubt you'll be next though.

Peter and I then travelled up to Whitby for the weekend – glorious weather – and then back to work as usual on the Monday. We've got a couple of very important pitches coming up soon. It's just as well as I'm becoming a little worried about business. Two of our major accounts sought Agencies elsewhere – not through any fault of our own, but because they decided that after four years with us they needed fresh, new ideas. If the worst comes to the worst I can always take up modelling full time and supplement it with temp work. I really admire the work you do. That really is a commitment. Oh by the way, I did find out. Sheffield Poly do some studies into retarded behaviour and mental handicap so you could always write there when you've finished your training. I will try and pop up to the Open Day next month – could you tell me which ward you're on? In fact, if there's anything in the fund raising line, etc., that you'd like me to do, or even organize, then you know you just have to shout.

I made my first appearance last Saturday as Miss Leeds United. Needless to say they lost. In fact they haven't won any of their first five matches. I really do think I have an ill effect on business! Maybe I should have done teaching after all. I enjoyed myself all the same. If you're ever free, I do get a spare ticket for the Director's box so do come. Plenty of handsome footballers – problem is they're usually on the other side, i.e. the away team!

How's the weight problem now. I've discovered a marvellous new method of losing weight. Anu, the friend of mine who owns a jewellery shop in Chiswick, drinks the juice of one fresh lemon daily. She hasn't cut down on anything else and has managed to lose, would you believe, 17 pounds in less than four months. I've tried it. If I cut down I don't lose weight but if I eat more I don't seem to put weight on either. My metabolism must be set. I thought I must be about 9 stone although when I was at the badminton club I weighed myself there and it said 8½. So pleased, was I, I had two packs of crisps and a bar of chocolate. So now I feel thoroughly depressed.

My next job today is to nip down to the RSPCA in Leeds to rescue a couple of kittens for the house. I'm very excited about it.

Any ideas for any names?

Send me a letter as soon as you can re the Open Day at the hospital won't you. And remember, 1st week in October, new house!!! What fun!

Until then take care.

Much love,
Hilary

(Hilary Ann Turner)

Dearest FP,

I *had* to write. I had the most extraordinary experience this morning: I met a woman who used to be a man. I went round to see her at the request of a friend of D's. She is in need of help compiling notes for what she intends to be the bestseller about her life and I said I'd have a chat with her.

Is it pure revisionism to say that one's sexual identity must be the most fundamental and powerful part of one's sense of self? Are you screaming? I don't believe that that is incompatible with everything feminism has been saying for the last umpteen years (or indeed what we sat up too late every night saying with E and S in the old flat). I suppose I just feel after meeting this woman that you had better be pretty firmly rooted in your sexual identity and *then* work on all those things you obviously have so much in common with the opposite sex.

The other thing which occurs to me *once again* is what an extraordinarily delicate interplay it is between social acceptance and self acceptance that produces the well-balanced individual. You wouldn't think nature would have relied on so tenuous a process when working on the success of our species. But then maybe all human beings (and not just trans-sexuals) are freaks for that very reason. This woman has spent her (his?) whole life feeling alienated from himself and so now at the age of seventy (!) has had a sex change – presumably in his desperate desire to *belong* – and has succeeded only in finally alienating himself from the rest of the world.

Or is that only *my* perception of what has happened because, as a result of all my own prejudices, I couldn't accept this individual simply as a fellow creature just because he/she has been both man and woman. That of course brings us on to how nothing and no one (arguable) exists in a vacuum but only really exists in another person's perception and contact with them so that what your relationship is is always much bigger than the sum of both your parts (pause for breath).

This of course gets us rather rapidly on to God and the cosmos – and all because some not very interesting former manager of a draper's shop in Northampton has had his willie chopped off.

And that in frightfully elegant fashion gets me right back to my first point, viz. if the chopping off of a penis can get me so bloody fast to God, *is* sexual identity truly the most basic of all human characteristics – and one which doesn't bear too much tampering with? Is there something almost inexplicable which separates the sexes?

We know of course though that all of this is tosh because ultimately I have more *in common* with this woman than things (like chopped-off willies) that separate us: the desire to be warm, comfortable, loved – feel useful – have a few laughs, all that we share.

The whole visit veered in rather dizzying fashion from the quite profound to the perfectly banal. She lives alone in a depressing-as-only-the-British-can-do-it post-war bungalow. It's pretty dingy. There's a bust of Churchill on the mantelpiece surrounded by pink-faced dolls in wedding dresses. When I first walked up to her door I really thought she made quite a convincing, attractive older woman wearing impeccable make-up (eye-lashes dyed blue) and an outfit rather in the style that predominates among woman who think they're dressing like the Queen.

The thing is – as the morning progressed she looked more and more like a man to me. I was riveted every time she hoisted herself out of her chair. She's elderly after all and not the least bit delicately built. Was it the missing willie – or the place where it had once been – that I – worldly old me – was on the look out for?

She (when she was a he) was married twice (never had sex with either woman!), began to cross dress about five years ago and had the op last year. I found her talk just a little disconcerting as all she wanted to discuss (with me, a total stranger) were her sexual feelings and I couldn't decide whether that was quite acceptable (as it was obviously such a relief to her to be having what she clearly has always imagined as a 'girl' talk) or whether it was the most pornographic event I'd ever taken part in in my life.

There I was, for Lord's sake, in a strange suburb with a large rather odd-looking lady, dressed as if for the Tory Party Conference, talking about the pros and cons of vibrators!

Seriously, part of the problem does seem to be that men who become women (is that actually possible?) seem to crave those aspects of 'womanhood' that anyone sensible I know has long since rejected – or at least got into perspective – like: laying out one's see-through pink négligé, doing the old fingernails, flirting with waiters, waiting for someone to open the door for you.

Ultimately, however, what is so awful about her situation is that she must have expected so much to change after she finally became a woman but really all the human problems remain: she's elderly, alone and without a lot of money. She wants a mate, she wants to travel. She wants for life not to be over – and what could be more purely and recognizably like you and me and everyone else than that? And yet I was uncomfortable – and still am. Because she was neither one thing nor the other, there was an extraordinary barrier between us. Interesting, don't you think?

Write immediately with all your thoughts otherwise I shall be cross – and we can't do with two bad correspondents in this relationship.

Love,
RW

(Rebecca Waters)

Welcome to Briary Cottage!!

How we wish we could have been here ourselves to 'introduce'
you to our lovely home, sorry what used to be *our* lovely home.
It's now yours, and may all the luck we had within these walls,
pass on to you. From the estate agent, I believe you are a young
engaged couple, so I can only imagine how thrilled you must be to
have just turned the key in the front door for the first time. I
remember when Martin and myself did the same thing – millions
of years ago – or so it seems.

Of course, the 'Briary' doesn't look now as it did then, nor did
it tell as much of a tale, but one thing you can be sure of, this has
been a wonderfully happy home, full of love, and always filled
with laughter, but most of all – just 'home'. Wait until some
evening, when you are both coming home thoroughly exhausted,
and you turn in through the twin chestnut trees (which, I might
add, we planted on our first wedding anniversary some 48 years
ago), and you behold its whitewashed walls and its oak door just
pleading to be pushed open. Oh, how we loved this house!!

I remember when it was just another cottage down Cornhill
Lane, and, as the name suggests, covered with blackberry
bushes. When Martin had proposed to me, we went looking for a
'suitable' house in which to set up home, and well, here we are, or
rather, *were*. Mind you, there was no water indoors, nor back
boiler to heat what was then only three rooms.

The bathroom and the kitchen are both recent additions. By
'recent' I mean when God decided to bless us with five children
we *had* to build on – like, about 35 years ago. Our children had
the heating installed for us for our Ruby Anniversary present, so
it's reasonably new. What a luxury it was for us! It helped
Martin's chest complaint during the winter months these last few
years. Little did we realize that the self-same ailment would force
us to warmer climates. My word, reading back on this letter, you
are getting more *our* life history than that of the cottage. Well, I
suppose they're both so closely entwined that it's difficult, or well
nigh impossible, to differentiate between them.

There's not much more I can add at this stage. We sincerely

wish you both a really happy future together, and hope that the love and joy you feel today will stay with you, as it did with us, for the rest of your married lives.

Good Luck,
Martin and Elizabeth Donnelly

PS If you happen to be digging in the back right hand-corner of the garden, and come across what look suspiciously like human bones, don't panic!! You'll have happened upon the official resting place of the numerous dogs, cats and sundry other pets who shared our 'castle'.

Dear Jane,

At last I've found the independence I'd been striving for. I cut the umbilical attachment to my mother's plates of lasagne and home-made flapjacks, and found a one-roomed bedsit that bears a closer resemblance to a dog kennel than somewhere to live, eat, sleep and shave your legs.

Three paces takes you from cooker to television (black and white, without a horizontal hold). Another four paces and you stumble over my bed/settee (unmade and uncomfortable). A further two strides to the left and you're out of the front door and into the hallway. The only advantage of living within such a restricted zone is my ability to get ready for work with the minimal amount of effort. By simply pivoting on my right foot I can wash, get dressed, make coffee, watch breakfast TV and bring in the milk. Sounds fun? It isn't.

The immediate view through my smoke-stained net curtains, that incidentally came free with the room, is yet another set of smoke-stained net curtains in the opposite flat. Beneath me, red buses cough out wisps of exhaust fumes as they lethargically crawl along the road, and an assortment of bodies carefully steps over unwanted take-aways that decorate the street.

I know I'm moaning, Jane, but bedsit land just isn't what I believed it might be. Remember how we visualized intelligent conversations with interesting neighbours, late-night parties and new-found friends constantly calling round for coffee? Well I'm still waiting for my first visitor (excluding the Jehovah's Witness who persistently rang my door bell last night). And the only conversation I'm managing to hold is with my rubber plant. Even that's decided to shed its leaves and slowly die. I think it overdosed on Baby Bio.

Independence in reality is symbolized by a lone egg in the solitude of an empty fridge, nights out at the launderette and a purse that yearns to feel the splendour of paper money. And I do despise watching my landlord readily snatch £30 of my hard-earned cash each week with a swifter movement than a Venus Fly Trap.

What about the neighbours, you may ask? Well the couple downstairs worship the gospel according to Blake and Crystale Carrington. In just three weeks I have learnt to recognize every voice that ever muttered a word on American Soap Opera. I don't think they've discovered volume control on their TV set. They are convinced I'm abnormal just because I don't eat meat or read the *Sun*.

I am also forced to listen to a rhythmical creaking sound coming from the flat above as Antony (the occupant) indulges in his regular nightcap of female company. I politely tried asking him to sample Ovaltine or hot cocoa so I could snatch some undisturbed slumber. He refused and performed with even further vigour the following evening (for three hours. God I feel inadequate.)

I really think the whole world is out enjoying themselves except me. I've already devoured eight custard creams for comfort. And all that tomorrow promises is The Archers on Radio 4 followed by the sweet smell of freshly laundered clothes. An unfulfilling hour watching a multitude of colours spin round and round as I search the launderette in hope of an unwanted newspaper. So empty is my life that a good weekend for me means finding an intact Sunday supplement.

Actually I was invited round to Antony's tonight for a meal. I was tempted. Not by Antony but the thought of real food and not the prepackaged junk I've grown accustomed to. The kind of meals that shout 'monosodium glutomate' just when you've decided to change to a high-fibre, additive-free diet. (I'm still convinced that bran should only be fed to horses and cattle.) However, I refused his invite believing the evening would end with the inevitable question, 'Coffee, your couch or mine?'

I know I should be practising self-assertion (I've read more than enough articles on the subject). I could take myself to the cinema, theatre, wine bar or restaurant. The choice is mine. But the only thing I feel capable of achieving at the moment is munching the very last custard cream in the packet. By the time you reach the 12th biscuit they don't taste so bad. Thank heavens for stretch jeans though.

Perhaps in another month or so I may have adjusted to this new deprived lifestyle and stopped pining for some home comforts and old friends. But before I finish this 'I'm-feeling-sorry-for-myself letter', I must ask you one small favour. If you do happen to see my mother, please tell her I am having a wonderful time.

Love, kisses and custard creams,
Julia

Dear Sue,

I can't get you on the phone so I'm importuning you by letter to let me come and stay with you for a few days. I have just spent a long weekend with my mother in the country, supposedly on a repairing lease while my flat is being decorated, and my nerves are in tatters.

'Come down for some peace and fresh air,' she trills, 'away from all the noise and chaos of London.' Well, believe you me, the boot is well and truly on the other foot.

I drove down on Thursday night, arriving after dark. About half a mile short of the cottage, rounding a particularly sharp bend, I come to a screeching halt inches away from a white blob standing in the middle of the road. This turns out to be a sheep which has escaped from a neighbouring field and can't find its way back in. Mindful of the considerable investment riding on each woolly back, I turn my car into a mechanized sheep-dog and finally persuade it to rejoin the flock. By this time I am more than ready for bed but there is still one hitch; Mother has retired leaving the key on the inside of the lock. The bell proved useless so I was forced, with the car as a disapproving onlooker, to hurl pebbles at her window for a considerable time until she finally surfaced and came down to let me in.

'Now you have a nice rest, dear. Stay in bed as long as you like.' Fateful words. I am awoken about 5 the following morning by a nasal voice repeating 'Sit!' in commanding accents. I crawl to the window and peer out with jaundiced eye, to discover it is our parrot trying to do a Barbara Woodhouse on the cat. Sarah came from a household where they were training a dog and is, apparently, unable to distinguish between feline and canine, much to the annoyance of the cat who hates to be told to do anything.

Further sleep seemed impossible since birds, farmyards and tractors had all started their day, so I went downstairs determined to do as little as possible. The rest of the day passed fairly peacefully if you discount 2 power saws starting up just over the hedge (they're cutting down the forest between the cottage and the reservoir so I think they may be there some time). Oh and a visit from the Jehovah's Witnesses who insisted on us buying both their magazines and lectured us on the imminence of

Armageddon. I begin to believe them, but I doubt whether becoming a member of the Faithful will in any way avert it!

That evening I returned early, hoping to snatch a night's rest before the wildlife awoke. At about 1 a.m. I became dimly aware that the power saws had started up again. 'Surely not' I groaned before full consciousness took over and I realized they could hardly operate in the pitch black. Anyway this terrible roar seemed to grow and subside in overlapping waves. I heard Mother in the corridor so enquired sweetly if she could account for it.

'Yes, it's those damnable scramblers I'm afraid. They use the lane for their rallies as they can keep going round the circle. Infuriating but there's nothing to be done as it's a public highway with no speed limit.'

'How long are they likely to keep it up?'

'Until one of them wins; I'm not sure how long that takes. However there's a very interesting play on the World Service if you'd care to join me in my room...'

Saturday I did not attempt to go out. The day was hot and still and the power saws silent but the gardener had come to cut the grass, an all-day event. He sweated and laboured so much, I couldn't bring myself to be seen lazing in the vicinity. Added to which the machine was far from silent. Mother was weeding at the back but I kept to my room. In the late afternoon I was just falling into a deep sleep when a commotion started in the orchard. I tried to ignore it but soon the back door opened and Mother hailed me. Went downstairs to discover 2 elderly ladies in a very distressed condition, wearing large sunhats tied under their chins and gulping our whisky. They had apparently gone for a walk in the forest, not the bit they're cutting down, lost their bearings and roamed around all day convinced they'd never get out. When they did it was unfortunately into our orchard. I was elected to drive them back to where they *thought* they'd left their car. They hadn't, in fact, but we found it eventually and I slunk home to stare gloomily at the depleted bottle.

The Sabbath was now my only hope. Surely, I thought, the country being a conservative place, quiet and peace would reign on a Sunday. The weather was beautiful so I took a lounger out under the pear tree and surrendered myself to SLEEP...

But soon came 'put, put, put', the sound of a motor scooter

coming up the drive. Then footsteps, then conversation. It was a young lad from the village who does odd jobs for Mother and they were discussing the rival merits of the village pubs. There was some confusion over the lower pub only having 'free' people in it of an evening which Mother took to mean they served 'free' beer rather than it was very poorly patronized but all was eventually sorted out. Mother then went away and the lad began energetically smashing glass with which to scrape down the front door to the loud accompaniment of Radio 1.

It is now Monday morning and I shall rush into the village with this and catch the first post. Please don't fail me dear friend. I know your flat is just off Piccadilly Circus but, believe me, that will be heaven after a weekend in the country!

Your loving friend,
Pauline